Hannelore Goos

Divine Messengers

Roman Roots of Astrological Planet Symbols

© 2016-2019
Printed and published by: BoD – Books on Demand, Norderstedt.
ISBN: 978-3-7494-0822-1

Content

Originally Latin words are typed in small capitals because minuscles were not used before the 8th century AD.

Foreword

Until the second part of the 20th century the planets of our solar system were designated with Roman (Latin) names of antique deities. With low adjustments these names are in all languages of the western world identical.

But if someone wishes to know who these gods and goddesses have been, whose names are thus used, an astonishing phenomenon can be observed: Traditional portrayals in literature do not present Roman deities but their so-called Greek equivalents.

This isn't found in respect of any other ancient religion: Seeking information about Egyptian gods the Egyptian mythology is presented, for Sumerian, their pantheon, questions about Germanic Religion are mostly answered from the Icelandic Edda. Even Indian or African deities are described in connection to their native religions. Only Roman gods and godesses are defined by Greek myths.

This could be ignored if names would be only haphazard combinations of letters without special own meanings. Traditional customs show that this is not true: Women used to change their family name when they got married, nuns and monks choose a new name when accepting the orders – these are only two examples for changing the name according to a change of life circumstances. From shamanism and ritual magic the concept is reported that someone can get power on everything and everybody whose (secret) true name he knows.

Hence, names have a meaning for the name bearer, especially names of divinities, of whom it is suggested that they have been called out many thousand times daily during the era of their worship. In respect of Roman cult we have to notice that not all gods and goddesses had Latin names: Isis stayed Isis (Egyptian) and Apollo stayed Apollo (Greek), just two examples to mention. Yet, the Romans had names and special cults for those deities which are today still used as planetary names. This justifies the question who was really identified this way.

In astrology a description of planetary symbols usually starts from the premise that there exists a correspondence between the symbolic contents and the eponymous myths. In many astrological books this connection is used for the explanation and clarification of planet symbols. But while Latin planet names corresponding to Roman deities are used, Greek mythology is narrated. Related science today rejects the old view that gods and goddesses of Romans and Greeks would be identical.

Nomen est Omen – not only from numerology we know that names transport spiritual content as well. When Roman gods are called to name planetary symbols, the involved subtexts cannot be identical with Greek ones. So it makes sense to incorporate Roman religion into the explanations of planet symbols. But native Roman religion is professional knowledge of only a handful of specialists in Roman history and religion.

Name equivalents for Mercury as example:

Latin	MERCURIUS
German	Merkur
English	Mercury
French	Mercure
Russian	Merkurij

1

Therefore one of this book's intentions consists in collecting information about those gods who are perpetuated in planet names until modern days and present it in a readable form for everybody. For astrologers this will enhance practical daily work by enriching the comprehension of planet symbols and thus optimising their interpretive skills. The Romans with their superficial INTERPRETATIO ROMANA called deities of different pantheons identical by just regarding a handful of responsibilities, attributes or character traits.

This idea seems to have survived centuries and might have been one of the roots of Carl Gustav Jung's concept of psychological archetypes. He explains these resemblances as the result of universal prototypes for ideas that exist independently from a specific civilisation in every human. His theory transports in this way, not only the medieval Christian opinion that heathen gods are not entities but human imaginations, but also the concept of effective equality of deities with more or less corresponding attributes and spheres of competence. Religious scholars nowadays regard this position by all means obsolete.

Carl Gustav Jung (1875–1961), Swiss psychiatrist and founder of analytic psychology, advanced the concept of psychological archetypes. Jung defined archetypes as universal, archaic patterns and images that derive from the collective unconscious. They are autonomous and hidden forms which are transformed once they enter consciousness and are given particular expression by individuals and their cultures. Being unconscious, the existence of archetypes can only be deduced indirectly by examining behaviour, images, art, myths, religions, or dreams. C. G. Jung deduced the existence of archetypes from astrology, alchemy, comparative religious science, dreams, fairy tales, legends and myths.

And if gods are respected as real discreet entities this point of view is completely wrong. The insufficiency of some resemblances as a proof for the same person is illustrated in a little story by GardenStone:

> "The two names Fritz and Fred are both derived from ,Friedrich' and etymologically this comes from ,fridu and ,rihi'. It means something like ,ruler who maintains peace and protects against force of arms'.
>
> Fritz resides near Munich in Germany and Fred in York in UK. They are of equal age and look as if they were twins. Both were graduated from high schools with the same notes and got a job as a banker. They are both married, have two children, whose mother has fiery red hair. Both believe in god, but on Sunday they don't go to church, perhaps because they like to spend a lot of time in the weekends on flea markets where they especially look for old books about cars. In their leisure time they both prefer wearing black clothes and love to play loud symphonic folk metal music. On the workdays each of them drives in their dark blue Renault the 20 miles to work. Nevertheless, the Munich guy is not identical with the one from York, they even don't know each other."

(The Mercury-Woden-Complex, p. 154)

If it turns out that the Roman gods and goddesses are more in accordance with modern astrological symbols than their Greek predecessors an important deficiency has to be stated: Comparable mythological narratives about them do not exist. But in Germany there is a modern story teller who has already tried to fill the gap …(see literature list, Antonio Cuoco)

Who were in fact the Romans?

In history books the content matter usually is presented as fact and proven information. In truth a good many courses of events are still unknown. We cannot say where the Sumerians came from, there are only hypotheses. Who were the Etruscans? The Romans have mythicized their origin themselves – everybody knows the tale of Romulus, Remus and the she-wolf, that is an invented myth and says little about the real ancestry of the town inhabitants.

In trying to find the original content of the Roman religious world it is necessary to determine the people(s) and cultural heritage of those who as "Romans" conquered a gigantic empire, starting in one single town. They influenced and influence all European civilisations till nowadays, but their origination and roots are still veiled behind the myths they created themselves.

Going back to the time, that is said to be Rome's founding period by later authors, we find, fairly verified by archaeological record, that on each of the "seven" hills forming the later town there was a small settlement of huts – laid out as high as possible because the low ground in between was regularly flooded by the Tiber and therefore swampy. In the Palatine Museum in Rome a model of such a hut village can be seen.

On occasion of excavations in 1948 remnants of three huts were found, including ground plans and holes for the piles which carried the roofs; walls obviously had been made by a mixture of clay and straw. Burial places which could be dated to 10th–8th century BC were found nearby.

These hill villages seem to be inhabited by people of different tribal membership: On the Palatine Hill Latines, on Esquilin, Viminal and Quirinal Sabines. There are presumptions that there were Sabellics, Lulanes and Hirpines as well, because the totem animal of these tribes was the wolf which plays an important role in the later composed founding myth of the town.

Palatine Museum

The Palatine is the hill where, according to tradition, Romulus founded Rome in 753 BC: the remains of huts confirm in full the details of the legend. Currently situated within the palace of the Caesars is the Palatine Museum, where the most important finds of the excavations are on display. The museum was founded in 1882 by the French Emperor Napoleon III.

Model of a reconstructed hut settlement on Palatin Hill,
approx. 8th century BC, Palatin museum

LUPERCALIA (see p. 80)
was a festive ritual in which young men girded only with a goatskin ran through the city. Women who presented themselves in their way, were beaten with fur strips on their hands; this should bring fertility and pregnancy. But the meaning of this ceremony was already unknown in republican times. Presumably, it is the remains of an archaic initiation rite. (Ulf)

Common mnemonic to remember the names of the seven hills of Rome: "Can Queen Victoria Eat Cold Apple Pie?" (Capitoline, Quirinal, Viminal, Esquiline, Caelian, Aventine, and Palatine)

Titus Livius

(about 59 BC–17 AC), in English called Livy, Roman historian and author under the reign of Augustus intended to write a comprehensive Roman history called AB URBE CONDITA, wherein he compiled official heritage with common oral traditions.

Capitol Hill is told to be used as burial place of several settlements until the construction of monumental buildings in Etruscan style. The influence of this people becomes obvious by the folk memory of three "Etruscan" kings reigning from the end of the 7th century BC. They organized the agglomeration of settlements following structures of Etruscan towns and formed a city administration accordingly. During this time immigration of individual families from the Greek cities south of present-day Naples is recorded.

The terms of cooperation practised by the hill villages reflect the special Roman pragmatism already in this early stage. On one hand they were united by a loose Community of worship, which was characterized by two rituals: The LUPERCALIA described on the left and the SEPTIMONTIUM on Dec 11th (feast of the seven hills), associated with these peaks: Oppius, Palatium, Velia, Fagutal, Cermalus, Caelius and Cispius, which do not comply with the later official "seven hills of Rome". Because of its age the SATURNALIA (p. 95) can be ranked among immemorial community festivals as well.

On the other hand, the villages worked only together when a major task had to be dealt with, such as the construction of a cart road to the market, led through the swamp of the so-called VELABRUM between the Capitol and the Palatine, which was finally drained only in the Imperial period.

However, the most important resource of this settlement site was a much-frequented Tiber ford, not only used by shepherds, but also by the salt caravans of the Etruscans on their way from the sea to the hinterland. The left riverbank at this point formed a market-place that still in reported Roman times was used as a cattle market (FORUM BOARIUM).

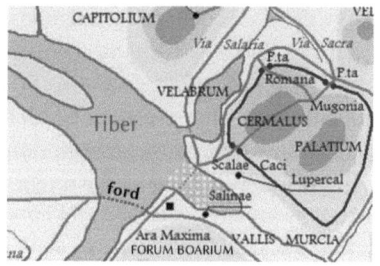

Rome in the founding time. Tiber ford dotted.

Such a trading place of course always attracts a wide variety of people, and when a nearby countryside is fit for colonization they remain. So it cannot be excluded that individual Phoenicians too discovered the lucrative place and may have settled there permanently. Hence the area, which will later be the city of Rome, was an early meeting point and melting pot of many different cultures. Additionally there was a sanctuary as reported by Livy (AB URBE CONDITA 1.8), where all sorts of more or less evil people gathered from elsewhere, exiles as well as runaway slaves and criminals.

How a major city could derive from this loose association is still in dispute. There is the theory of a city founding passed down from the myths, but not verified by archaeological finds – traces of a real city wall are not detectable before the 4th century BC, its construction therefore was a response to the "Celtic Storm" in the year 387 BC, the conquest and looting of the city. The other hypothesis assumes a continuous city development, a quasi-natural coming together by population growth and immigration from the surrounding Latins and Etruscans.

Anyway, around the year 600 BC, Rome was hostess at an annual meeting of the "Latin League", a local coalition of about 30 urban communities, and thus certainly recognised as a city among cities. About a hundred years later the establishment of 300 GENTES took place, family clans, whose representatives formed the people's assembly (Senate) and chose the ruling Consuls.

Whoever was born on the territory of the city of Rome or belonged to one of the GENTES, was Roman citizen and therefore Roman, externally recognizable from 200 BC on by three names:

	First name	family name	personal name
e. g.	GAIUS	JULIUS	CAESAR.

A special ethnicity was not considered.

To the Latins Rome felt connected still for a long time, the members of this people had unlike other peoples outside the city advanced rights and the "Latin" feasts stayed state holidays until imperial times. Even the language of the Romans, Latin, LINGUA LATINA, has its roots in the languages of the Latin tribes, though it evolved a good deal later. Latin script, however, is a combination of Etruscan and Greek characters, which shows clearly, from which directions cultural impulses invaded the Roman society. On the question of who actually were the Romans, there is only the simple answer: Men with Roman citizenship, especially the residents of the city of Rome. By descent they were a mixture of all peoples inhabiting central and southern Italy in the last millenium BC.

And where remain Romulus and Remus and their wolven fostress? As already mentioned, the narrative description concerns a myth, which was noted centuries later. It resembles the Greek myth of Amphion and Zethos (twin brothers, half gods, repudiated, drawn up by a shepherd, founders of the city of Theben), only the she-wolf was added – possibly with reference to the VER SACRUM described on p. 64. Thus it is conceivable that the story was initially invented as Greek poetry, which served the purpose of representing the city, emerging as a power factor, as influenced by MAGNA GRAECIA, the coastal areas of southern Italy on the Tarentine Gulf that were extensively colonized by Greek settlers (also by recourse to Aeneas). Later, the Romans were only too happy to adopt this homemade story in order to legitimize their special position among the cities of Italy.

Considering, that the later Romans in the early days settled on hilltops, to escape, especially in summer, the steaming heat and mosquitoes of the marshes in between, a demarcating furrow drawn with the plough around the main settlement seems very unlikely.

Only flat country inhabitants can have invented the legend of this PRIMIGENIUS SULCUS, which Romulus is said to have pulled; at stony mountain-slopes something like that was not at all possible.

On 22 June 2013 the Roman daily paper "Corriere della Sera" announced what had been assumed already for a long time in the professional world: After radio carbon investigations of the Italian University of Salento it is proved that the so-called "Capitoline Wolf" is not an Etruscan bronze, but originates from a medieval counterfeiter's workshop of the 11. – 12. Century.

Since after the pillaging in 387 BC, practically no record has remained from ancient times, the fiction from oral tradition was happily recorded as sugar-coated history.

Later generations and all classical philologists in Europe took the beautiful legends as quasi factual descriptions. It was seldom questioned: The city of Rome was inhabited permanently, layer over layer was constantly built there since antiquity, therefore archaeological investigations are difficult even with today's methods. Earlier generations could not doubt the mythological narrations.

But in the meantime modern historical scientists succeeded in bringing a little light into the early period of the city and its inhabitants that is so immensely important for the European culture.

And in such a way we know now at least in general terms, who were the Romans.

This section is based in particular on the following literature, where further information can be found:

Aigner-Foresti, Luciana, Die Etrusker und das frühe Rom, 2. Auflage, Darmstadt 2009.

Alföldi, Andreas, Das frühe Rom und die Latiner, Darmstadt 1977, German translation of "Early Rome and the Latins", University of Michigan Press 1965.

Forsythe, Gary, A Critical History of Early Rome, London, 2005.

Roman Religion

The origin of the subdivision into literary, philosophical and political or state religion is ascribed to the Roman historian Varro. However reading scientific treatises on Roman religion from the 18th and 19th centuries (for example Maternus, Preller, see bibliography p. 109), you will notice quickly, that there is no distinguishing between the different traditions. Greek-influenced literature and philosophy is mixed with elements of Roman folk religion and state cult. The result was a widespread (and still remaining) perception that Roman and Greek religion followed the same pattern, only the names of the divinities were adapted to the respective languages. But this does not describe the real cult practises Rome maintained until the late imperial period.

From the genesis of the 'multicultural' city of Rome it can be assumed, that the world of Roman gods and goddesses does not consist of a pantheon of connected or related natures. The cults of the individual ethnic groups and tribes remained partially, partly they mixed. From outside new deities were added. All existed side by side, there was no creation story, no myth of origin, no descent from each other and no marriages. Even a heaven (Olympos) as an abode of the gods and an underworld is missing in original Roman religion. Unlike the Greek pantheon, the Roman gods were not 'humanized'; only from the time of Etruscan influence were statues made of them. These figures served mainly decorative purposes. Gods were by virtue of their will and action (their NUMEN) always present, had their attributes and responsibilities and made known their intentions by special signals (NUMINA). It was the task of priestly augurs to read these signs (flashes, the flight of birds, animal intestines). The payment of the augurs was an important source of income for all temples. At this point there were early conflicts with the 'Chaldeans', astrologers from Mesopotamia who had migrated from there and offered their services in Rome for money (s. p. 16).

Gods and goddesses were entitled to their associated cultic actions; in return, the gods were responsible for advancement in the cult raised area. If this promotion didn't take place, the cult was not performed correctly. This emphasis on cultic acts meant that, unfortunately, of many deities only the name and their festivities are known, little or nothing however from their religious background or myths.

The origin of the Roman patchwork religion led also to the fact that the Romans were very tolerant towards other deities, especially those of conquered peoples. In early times the so called INTERPRETATIO ROMANA was used, which goddesses and gods simply equated because of external attributes. This then was expressed in double names such as MERCURIUS AVERNUS (several votive stones in Celtic and Germanic areas), MARS THINGSUS (revered by the Tubanti) and HERCULES MAGUSANUS (Magusanus was the major god of the Batavians).

MARCUS TERENTINUS **VARRO** REANITUS (116–27 BC) was a so-called poly historian who wrote 70 works in more than 600 books, which however, almost all were lost. Only quotations of other scholars are known. He wrote about theology in the (completely lost) ANTIQUITATES RERUM HUMANARUM ET DIVINARUM, a Roman cultural history, which the 'doctor of the church' Augustine was said to have quoted from.

The multi-ethnic city had three deities of war:
• Mars (Latine)
• Quirinus (Sabine)
• Bellona (Samnite).

Even poets, who transferred Greek mythology onto the Roman gods, got problems with their lack of relationship.
So was – following Greek mythology – the war god Ares a son of the sky queen Hera.
Her 'counterpart', the Roman goddess Juno, was however not married!
Thus the poetical story came into being, that Juno became pregnant with Mars by passing an Orchid.
(Ovid, Fasti 5, 229–260)

Not only single Deities, but the whole of the Greek pantheon was literally equated with Roman goddesses and gods during the 3rd and 2nd century BC. Whether there were Italic myths before that time can only be suspected. As scholars up to the 20th century took over these reinterpretations without comment, the search for traces of the original mythology of the Roman gods remains tedious.

In this way, at the time of the greatest expansion the pantheon of the Roman Empire consisting of more than 450 gods and goddesses stayed relatively manageable.

But factually the INTERPRETATIO ROMANA didn't care much for cultic or mythological contents. So, for example, the Greek titan Cronus was equated to the Roman god Saturnus – because both held in their hand a harpe (sickle-sword) as their attribute.

An additional feature of the Roman religious practice was the attitude that every act of worship is worth a counter-action of the addressed divinity, shown in the religious formula DO UT DES (I give, so that you give). So there is a myriad of votive stones, mini-altars, evident from their inscription that they were donated due to a previously sworn vow. For the god of shepherds Silvanus more than 1100 such votive altars were found. The principle was always alike (s. p. 32): The later founder made a promise in the temple of the respective deity, e. g. "If my commercial trip to England will be successful and I'll return healthy, I'll donate an altar to the goddess". If the desired result appeared the votive stone was ordered from a stone cutter provided with the appropriate inscription, the name of the donor and purpose of the vow, and marked with the formula V·S·L·M (VOTUM SOLVIT LIBENS MERITO = has his vow dutifully and gladly solved). Of course, only wealthy Romans could pay a stonemason, less affluent brought other sacrificial offerings which, however, have not survived the centuries. In our understanding of religion, such trade has little to do with piety, in the pragmatism of the Romans it was a natural expression of their RELIGIO which is explained by Cicero as a state of permanent awareness.

Indeed the Romans were convinced to be the most religious humans of the world; not only Cicero and Livius write this, also Greek historians such as Polybios, Poseidonios and Atheaios place value on this statement.

The entire life of a Roman was crossed by the service. The cults of the main gods were part of the nation, the most important rituals were carried out in public and the participation was an obvious civic duty.

Religion was not responsible for rules of conduct in the meaning of commandments for the individual. In this purpose on one hand a civil law, on the other hand the rules of the clan were established. Every individual belonged to such a clan.

It was the task of the urban upper priest (PONTIFEX MAXIMUS) to announce monthly the respectively feasts and holidays on a white board – a weekly day off, Sunday, only starting since the year 321 AD.

At the same time, these announcements fixed the length of the respective month, because this was not standardised in early Roman times; only after introduction of the Julian Calendar 45 BC it was no longer necessary to insert intercalary days as required.

Important occurrences were transferred at expiration into the so-called ANNALES MAXIMI, a kind of public records.

Nobody 'decided' for a particular faith, but everyone was automatically a member of the cult. Therefore, it was not a problem for the Romans, to belong to several 'religions' at the same time:

1. Private Religion

   The familiars, who protected the particular space and hearth as centre of the food preparation, were worshiped as household gods (PENATES). They existed for individual houses (cooker gods), neighbourhood, city quarters and as PENATES PUBLICI POPULI ROMANI for the whole city of Rome. Their public worship was partially intertwined with the cult of Vesta. In principle Penates were tied to 'their' place. Maybe for private homes they had the same meaning as the teraphím in Palestine, a connection to the Phoenicians would therefore be quite conceivable.

   The LARES were familiar spirits, representing the ancestors. They belonged to the kinship and could move also with it to another place. In contrast to this there were also Lares, which belonged to a certain place (LARES LOCI). In rich houses there were particularly decorated house altars named "Lararium" for the worship of these spirits.

   The worship of the Penates and Lares resulted from the family and the house in which someone lived. Responsible for the cult here was the PATER FAMILIAS or chief of the clan.

Lararium from Pompeji, 79 AD
Sacrificial altar, surrounded by two snakes as representatives of the LARES LOCI, above the altar an image of a pine cone and two eggs, on top a sacrifice scene, on the right a niche for figurines of the gods.

9

2. Automatically, by his status every citizen belonged to the official state religion (status means "member of a recognised GENS"). According to the city's history, places of worship were initially on each hill settlement. The first common places were the temples of Vesta, Saturnus and the Castores in the FORUM ROMANUM and a three-cells-temple on Capitoline Hill where Jupiter, Juno and Minerva were honoured by the patricians. As a counterpart, a temple of the Plebeians, who was consecrated to Ceres, Liber and Libera was on Aventine Hill.

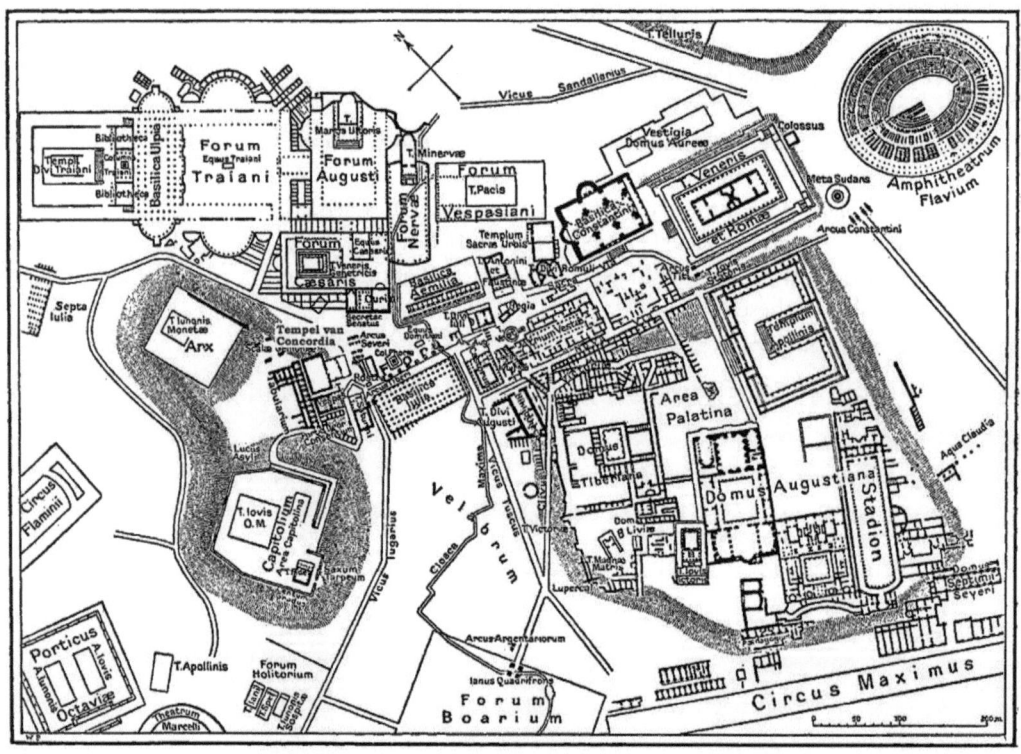

Map of the Roman cult places (engraving from 1916)

No later than in the 3rd century BC there existed a list of officially revered gods, the DEI CONSENTES based on Etruscan customs. In the Roman Forum, the center of the city, they stood as gilded statues in the PORTICO DEORUM CONSENTIUM, a particular temple designed in the form of a columned hall. It showed the following deities:

Name	Origin	Location(s) of the main temple(s)	Priest
Iuppiter	Latine	Capitol	FLAMEN DIALIS
Iuno	Etruscan	Quirinal, Capitol	REX SACRORUM
Minerva	Sabine	Capitol, Aventine	COLLEGIUM OPIFICUM
Mars	Latine	Field of Mars, Forum of Augustus	FLAMEN MARTIALIS
Venus	Phoenician	Roman Forum, Capitol	COLLEGIUM VENERIS GENETRIX
Vulcanus	Old-Italian	Roman Forum, Field of Mars	FLAMEN VOLCANALIS
Neptunus	Etruscan	Field of Mars	
Apollo	Greek	Palatine	
Diana	Latine	Aventine, Caelius, Esquiline	
Ceres	Old-Italian	Aventine	FLAMEN CEREALIS
Vesta	Old-Italian	Roman Forum	VIRGINES VESTALES
Mercury	Latine	Aventine	COLLEGIUM MERCATO-RUM

(FLAMEN, pl. FLAMINES)
Until the empire a collegium of 15 state priests was responsible for the official cult of the following deities:

IUPPITER
MARS
QUIRINUS
CARMENTA
CERES
FALACER
FLORA
FURRINA
PALATUA
POMONA
PORTUNES
VULCANUS
VOLTURNUS
and two, whose names are no longer known.

Before the republican period the kings had a double function: Secular regimen and high priest in religious ceremonies. When the governement moved to elected consuls, the institution of the REX SACRORUM (king of sacrifices) was established. He became the highest state priest residing in the REGIA, the former king's abode.

Remnants of the PORTICUS DEORUM CONSENTIUM in the Roman Forum

According to an inscription the building, from which originate these remains, was restored in the year 367 AD by the city prefect VETTIUS AGORIUS PRAETEXTATUS.

3. Miscellaneous cults

Other deities were worshipped by members of distinct profes-
sions (soldiers, shepherds, traders, artisans) or organisations
(brotherhoods). Temples, shrines and other cult places were
spread over the entire city.

There were very old ones f. i. for Mater Matuta and Portu-
nus in the Forum Boarium, the earliest commercial space. Also,
Hercules, god of the merchants was honored there with a shrine.

Spread across the city were places of worship of 'immigrant'
deities such as Faunus (or Fauna), Silvanus and Fortuna who
had moved there with their worshippers.

With the conquest of areas other than italic, the gods of
foreign countries came to Rome, especially the Isis, Cybele and
Mithras cult are to be mentioned here.

The diversity of the Roman religion meant that for a Roman the Imperial
cult (veneration of emperors) introduced since the assassination of Caesar
was no problem. Dead and later also living emperors were revered as gods,
temples built for them, and priests installed. This cult was one of the points
responsible for conflict with the Christians.

On the occasion of calendar reform of Julius Caesar the 7-days-week was introduced according to Babylonian and Egyptian models. Thereby the days of the week were named after the seven deities, to whom in Astrology celestial bodies are assigned:

Monday: DIES LUNAE
Tuesday: DIES MARTIS
Wednesday: DIES MERCURII
Thursday: DIES IOVIS
Friday: DIES VENERIS
Saturday: DIES SATURNI
Sunday: DIES SOLIS

This section is based in particular on the following literature, where further information can be found:

Müller, Volker, Römische Religionsgeschichte, Universität München, Fachdidaktik klassische Philosophie, WS 2010-11

Muth, Robert, Einführung in die griechische und römische Religion, 2. Auflage, Darmstadt 1998.

Dumezil, Georges, Archaic Roman Religion, translated from French by Philip Krapp, Baltimore 1996.

How astrology came to Rome

All pre-Roman civilizations of the ancient world conducted astronomy in one or the other form with the necessary observations of the sky. Since the New Stone Age humans depended on a prosperous agricultural production. This meant a time regulation for seed and harvest as successful as possible; therefore the production of a reliable calendar was the most important task. Moon and sun in its recurring positions gave here the corner marks.

Ales Stenar
Megalithic stone circle in southern Sweden, which is interpreted to have
served to determine the solstices.

In addition, all possible celestial phenomena were observed and inserted in different systems of divination. However, here only those are considered, in which the movements of sun, moon, planets and initially also some fixed stars are related to processes on earth. This means "astrology" since ancient times. Astronomy was a necessary auxiliary technique and has established itself as an independent science only in modern times.

We have the oldest astronomical data from the Sumerians. They observed first above all the moon, whose rhythm was easily comprehensible. The three-day time of new moon was particularly important as an interval timer. Also eclipses were observed, but not always distinguished between meteorological darknesses and astronomical eclipses.

To the sun the peoples of the near Orient had a split attitude: on the one hand it gave light and heat, on the other hand it could scorch the land and cause devastating droughts. But the myths collected by the ethnologist Frobenius show that only in the moderate climate the sun is felt as exclusively benediction-donating and therefore is female.

The important master clock in the sky is the moon.

It stands regularly after 29 days, 12 hours, 44 minutes and 2.9 seconds exactly between sun and Earth. Then it cannot reflect sunlight and appears black: The new moon. From this derived a month of 30 days.

The sun provided with the salient points
winter solstice
spring equinox,
summer solstice,
autumn equinox
the basis for the division of time during a year.

The term *astrology* = "knowledge of the stars" was created, because in the early days there was no differentiation between stars and planets – stars were everything that shone in the sky. Formerly the terms "fixed stars" and "wandering stars" were in use; together they formed the whole of celestial bodies.

Whether dense clouds or the shadow of the Earth darkened the Moon, both were a bad omen.

13

The Sumerians knew the planets Saturn, Jupiter, Mars and Mercury. That the Morning and Evening Star are both the same planet Venus was unknown; bright fixed stars like Sirius were also found in Sumerian astronomical records.

The constellation Cetus (Whale)

For the determination of the planetary motions it was important to define their place in the infinite night sky: For this purpose more and more stars were summarized to "pictures" (today constellations), in particular in the area of the sunrise exactly at east.

Some groups of stars were already interpreted as "constellations", such as Tiamat (today: Cetus/Whale). A regular twelve-parts zodiac did not yet exist however. Not the position of a sky light, but the timing of its emergence in the eastern sky (rising) and its appearance: light/dark, with or without corona etc. were the most important factors of the interpretation.

The prophet Daniel belonged to a group of Jewish prince children brought to the Babylonian royal court as hostages. It was usual, according to their rank, to educate them royally. This included training in the temple service and in astrology.

Despite his (for the Jews) 'heathen' activities Daniel remained faithful to Yahweh and became a prophet.

The Sumerians were also the first who assigned stars to certain gods. The movements of the heavenly bodies were interpreted as omens of the respective god's will. For individual humans in the sense of our current individual horoscopes there were however still no astrologically based predictions. The will of the gods deduced from the movement of the stars appeared on earth in good or bad weather, abundant crops or failed harvest, floods or drought, etc. Also, the course of reign of a king and the success or failure of a military expedition was read by the respected deity's priests. Astrology was part of religious worship and the training took place in temples. This was the cause of the prohibition of astrology for the Jews in the Old Testament, of which only the prophet Daniel was excluded.

The subsequent rulers of Mesopotamia built on the Sumerian conceptions, modified and supplemented them so that in late Babylonian time already an astrology in today's sense can be noticed. Former temple priests began to offer forecasts on astrological basis for payment at this time. Simultaneously, a permanent exchange of astrological knowledge with the neighbouring countries took place as usual.

The role played by the planets known at this stage of the astrological history, can be found on a cuneiform, the treaty between Esarhaddon, king of Assyria, and Ramataia, prince of the Medes from the 7th century BC. It says in the preamble:

"In the presence
- of the planets Sul.pa.ud.du (Jupiter), Dilbat (Venus), Kaimanu (Saturn), Gud.ud (Mercury), Dal.bat.a.nu (Mars), Sirius,
- and in the presence of Assur, Anu, Enlil, Ea, Sin, Shamash, Adad, Marduk, Nabu, Nusku, Urash, Nirgal, Ninlil, Sheru'a, Belet-ilani, mistress of the gods: Ishtar of Ninive und Ishtar von Arbela,
- by all the gods in [the cities of] Assur, Nineveh, Kalah, Arbela, Kakzu, Harran, by all the gods of Assyria, by all gods in, Borsippa, Nippur, by the gods of Sumer, all of them, by the gods of the lands, all of them; by the gods of heaven and of earth."

(Laessoe)

The Greeks were the first who distinguished the celestial objects by their movements, not by brightness.

Thus Sirius was ruled out, although it shines much brighter than most of the planets.

Contrary to popular conceptions it is evident from the text that the planets do not have the status of gods, they are clearly distinguished from the latter.

Their role is indicated by the translation of the name for Venus "herald". Hence, the planet announced by its appearance the will and intention of its associated deity. The this way constituted parallel between celestial and terrestrial manifestations without the planets being causing agents seems rather modern.

Cuneiform contract found in the ruins of Calah along the upper Tigris River near Nineveh

Enlarged section of the left fragment

The astrological doctrine of correspondence between celestial and terrestrial processes thus traces back to Sumerians and Babylonians.

Besides political also individual astrology was first practised in the cities of Mesopotamia. After in the Neo-Babylonian Empire of the Chaldeans from 625 BC on, the state religion lost its importance, the astrologer-priests had to open up new sources of revenue. They did not stay in their traditional countries, but moved with the offer "to be able to read the future" especially to the west and reached Egypt, Greece and Rome. Even after Persians, Alexander the Great and the Seleucid kings had taken over power in Mesopotamia, the name "Chaldean" for astrological working soothsayers remained.

Greek philosophers and scientists however were those, who on the one hand put Astrology on a scientific basis, but on the other deified the planets, as can be read in Plato's "Timaeus".

Observing the sky just before sunrise had led to the definition of eleven constellations that obviously formed a circle in the sky; these were Aries, Taurus, Gemini, Cancer, Leo, Virgo, Scorpio, Capricorn, Sagittarius, Aquarius and Pisces. Their skyway was called Zodíacos = "circle of living beings". Under influence of Mesopotamian astrology then the shears of Scorpio became another constellation which was taken over by the Greek natural philosophers. As already named by the Sumerians this constellation was called "Libra" (GIS-rin). The name zodíac was not changed even though the scale is not a living thing.

The English expression *zodiac* means a complete cycle, circuit or compass. [Middle English via Old French zodiaque and Latin zodiacus from Greek zoidiakos, from zoidion 'sculptured animal-figure', diminutive of zoion 'animal'(The Concise Oxford Dictionary, 9th Ed., 1995)

But already at that time it was recognizable that this (sidereal) zodiac is not permanently suitable for determining the position of celestial bodies, since it moves with the precession. Because of this, it is suggested, that, particularly with the help of Pythagoras, the **Tropical Zodiac** was developed. This is a kind of ethereal measuring tape which divides the annual way of the sun into 12 equal sections, at that time starting at the peak of the star at the end of the sign

The invention of the tropical zodiac can be ascribed plausibly to the Pythagoreans because they practised on the one hand mathematization and on the other hand mystification of the cosmos in their harmony of spheres.

Illustration for the Greek didactic poem PHENOMENA of ARATUS of SOLI,which describes the zodiac signs in the early 3rd century BC.

of Cancer (today at spring equinox in Aries). European astrology continued to develop using that tropical zodiac from now on for the definition of planet positions. This uniform system is valid today.

The Aristotelian doctrine of elements and temperaments was applied to the Zodiac segments, and thus the basis of modern Astrology came in existence – except for the planets. These were not only considered to be omens of the gods, but directly associated with deities as 'star of' Aphrodite or 'star of' Cronus, Hermes, Zeus, Mars. Sun and Moon lost their special role and were defined as belongings to Helios and Selene.

It must be taken into account in all these considerations that as a result of the empire Alexander the Great conquered, a lively exchange between the Babylonian, Egyptian and Greek science prevailed, so that it is partly no longer comprehensible, where which innovation was actually first introduced.

When the Marduk priest Berossos 280 BC founded an Astrologers school on the Greek island of Kos, to astrological tools aspect teaching was added, a little later it was supplemented with the astrological houses. So the common elements of astrology were all together at that time, there also were the first written planetary tables and even mechanical instruments illustrating sky constellations were constructed.

The spread of astrology was facilitated by the propagation of the philosophical doctrine of the Stoics who reduced everything happening in the world to a system of naturally proceeding laws based on a combination of physics and philosophy. Here, astrology and the in Babylon developed system of correspondences could be aligned excellently, so well, that some superficial critics claimed Stoics worshiped the zodiac instead of gods.

In particular, the Stoic Posidonius brought the view of astrology as natural philosophy to Rome, where his lectures were visited by Cicero and Pompeius. With the Stoic thoughts spreading in Rome the correspondence of celestial and terrestrial operations, the philosophical substratum of astrology, became a complement to the scientific bases. This point of view culminated in the "Meditations" laid down in Greek language by the Emperor Marc Aurelius, in which he notes:

> All things are implicated with one another, and the bond is holy; and there is hardly anything unconnected with any other thing. For things have been co-ordinated, and they combine to form the same universe [order] (Book VII, 9)

While the 'Chaldeans' (s. p. 16) acting as fortune-tellers were largely ignored by the educated Romans, Greek astrological writings brought about the turn. According to Thomas Schäfer these were brought to Italy especially 194 BC by the returning legions after the Roman-Syrian war.

The papers of the Hellenistic philosophers, mathematicians and natural scientists made astrology as a predicting system socially acceptable in upper class circles of Rome and partly replaced the divination systems of intestines

The Greek island of Kos had in antiquity a centuries-old tradition as a training centre. Here in the 5th pre-Christian century the most famous physician Hippokrates of Kos (460–370 BC) founded a medical school. His 'oath' belongs to the professional ethics of physicians still today

study, observation of birds flight and valuation of lightnings derived from the Etruscans. The first known astrologer who was trained completely in the "Hellenistic system" was the scholar and politician Publius Nigidius Figulus (around 100–45 BC). Following Lucan, he predicted among other things the victory of Caesar and the end of the republic. Mostly he is said to have dealt with weather astrology. Unfortunately his relevant writings are lost except fragmentary quotations by other authors.

From the beginning, however, the determinism that is often included in astrological forecasts was also point of criticism. In particular Cicero took over the arguments of the Greek sceptic Panaitios, some of which are still nowadays propounded by opponents of astrology. The main argument was, how it might be, if for every person in the individual horoscope an individual fate is recorded, that in the same moment the same fate happens to hundreds or thousands with natural disasters or wartime events. There are several invalidations of this argument, which can be found throughout the astrological standard literature.

Relief with Mithras from Neuenheim, 2nd century, Badisches Landesmuseum Karlsruhe, Zodiac pictures as frameworks

The astrological system of correspondences asserted itself especially in the Mithras cult. Mithraeae, veneration places of this god, were spread across Europe; they were placed aligned to astronomical constellations and decorated with zodiac images.

However, enemy attacks had no effect on the spread of astrology. Although it is unclear whether Julius Caesar employed it – supporters and opponents have woven stories about that, their substance is not verifiable. Be that as it may, since Emperor Augustus, the inclusion of astrological advice became usual in government decisions. Emperor Nero even issued coins shaped with his HOROSCOPUS (Ascendant) Capricorn.

At the same time the astrology of the 'Chaldeans' (s. p. 16) offered on markets was forbidden several times, unsuccessfully. In addition astrologers, who used their knowledge to predict in order to strike political capital from it, e. g. the end of a certain emperor, were pursued and threatened with heavy punishments. Except for the astrologers assigned by the emperor it was forbidden under penalty of death to 'read' the chart of the ruler. Nevertheless factionists of all directions repeatedly tried to use (or abuse) astrology for their own purposes. Contemporary 'astrologers schools', often were formed as close-knit communities based on a family clan, who tried to keep their knowledge secret from each other.

Different statements can be found why in the late Roman period Jupiter as the supreme god was replaced by SOL INVICTUS (Invincible Sun). Both the importance of Mithras as sun god and the spread of astrology are mentioned.

The Septizonium built by Emperor Septimius Severus (146–211 AD)

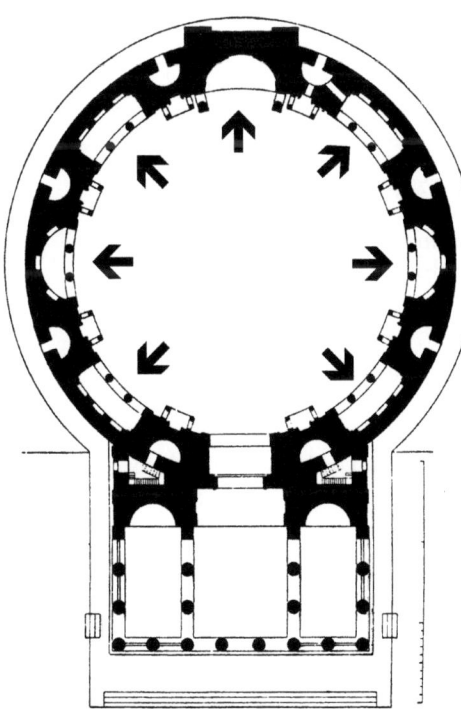

at the entrance to the Palatine Hill is said to be a building dedicated to the seven planets as gods. The form of the seven-day week with each day assigned to a planet, was finally introduced by Septimius. It is – except for a short period at the time of the French Revolution – still valid. Also the Pantheon building is linked to the 'planetary gods'.

Thus, astrology had finally arrived in the Roman Empire.

Floor plan of the Pantheon
In the seven niches statues of the seven planetary gods are said to have stood

While in the past the origins of Mithraism were seen in Persia, religious scholars nowadays think that it was a Greek mystery cult with Persian influence.
(according to Stuckrad)

The theory of astrological correspondences is summarized in the so-called "Hermetic Law", which is said to derive from the mythical Hermes Trismegistos:

"That which is Below corresponds to that which is Above, and that which is Above corresponds to that which is Below, to accomplish the miracle of the One Thing." (Scully p. 321)

Great innovations such as the introduction of the tropical zodiac by the Greeks 500 years earlier no longer took place, but the techniques were refined and in particular the individual astrology and chart reading experienced an unprecedented boom. All emperors had astrological consultants, even at a time when astrology was officially banned.

For the arising Christianity the stoical determinism was an anathema and so astrology in several council resolutions was lumped together with magic, Manichaeism and other heretical systems. But the reading of the divine will from 'signs in the sky' made no problems: after all, the Star of Bethlehem itself had announced the birth of the Saviour and that news arrived the astrologer-magicians in the East, who since the 6th century were honoured as the "Three Saint Kings " (the three biblical magi) from the 6th century on.

"Three Kings", ancient mosaic from Ravenna around 565.
The kings wear old-Persian traditional costume.

This section is based in particular on the following literature, where further information can be found:

Dietz, Otto Edzard, Geschichte Mesopotamiens von den Sumerern bis zu Alexander dem Großen, München 2004.

Lindsay, Jack, Origins of Astrology, London, 1972.

Schäfer, Thomas, Vom Sternenkult zur Astrologie, Düsseldorf 1993.

Stuckrad, Kocku von, Geschichte der Astrologie, Beck'sche Reihe, München 2007.

Astrological Symbols

Someone who uses a planet name nowadays, ostensibly does not really think of the Roman deity, who once shared this name. Astronomy and astrology are outwardly completely independent of the ancient religion, the names used don't have a religious meaning any more. But while in astronomy a planet name directly refers to the respective celestial body, it is used in astrology as astrological symbol, which denotes a multi- layered complex of senses. The planet name is a token for a network of interrelated meanings. Meanings belonging to a particular planet name are called rulerships, correspondences or, old-fashioned, signatures.

Through rulerships astrological symbols can be described. This is obtained for zodiac signs, planets (including sun and moon) and houses. The relationship between the symbols and their assignments may be understood better using a model.

Simplified, an astrological interpretation works by assigning a correspondence to each element recorded in a horoscope and then to combine the assignments among each other.

In this light rulerships can be defined as the basis of all astrological interpretations.

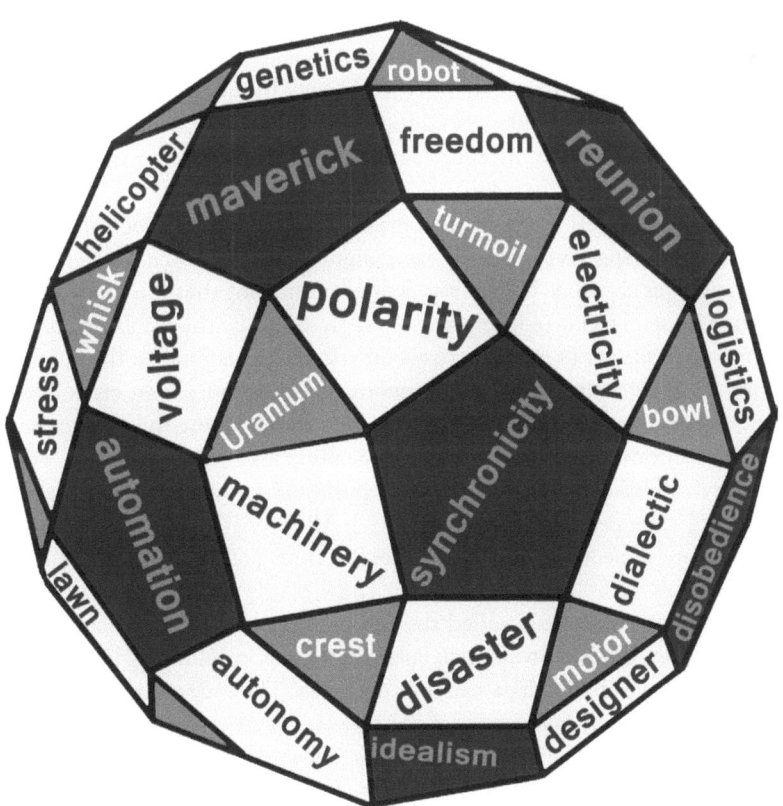

An astrological symbol can be imagined as a sphere with many facets; each corresponding term represents a facet:
As shown on the left, the characteristics belonging to the symbol can be imagined as printed on the respective facets.

Depending on from which side the body is looked at, one sees the symbol from another perspective, recognizes other rulerships, which refer however always to the same symbol; this is situated virtually 'invisible' in the centre of that ball.

Some rulerships of the astrological symbol Uranus as facet model

The definition of the astrological symbol results from the synopsis of the rulerships. Even though it shows many facets, the symbol is nevertheless always a whole, all its correspondences are subject to the same conditions at the same time.

Learning a language you have to learn vocabulary.

Learning astrology you have to learn rulerships.

The art of the astrologer lies in combining them accurately.

Already the cuneiform documents of Mesopotamia contain such correspondences, a fact which caused the religious scholar Koku Von Stuckrad to point out that certain interpretations in astrology did not change in their core for more than 2500 years (loc. cit. p. 61). And in the "Tetrabiblos" of Claudius Ptolemy (around 100–before 180), which was regarded till modern times as a standard work of western astrology, assignment lists are included which are intended to represent the symbolic meaning of each individual planetary and zodiacal sign principle. These catalogues were expanded to the so-called "Signature Doctrine" of Paracelsus (Theophrastus Bombastus of Hohenheim 1493–1541). In addition, the works of William Lilly (1602 –1681), father of English "Christian" astrology, contain such lists.

In this way Astrology has become a symbolic language. Everything that exists in the world, can be translated into this language by rulerships, its vocabulary consists of the correspondences for houses of the horoscope, zodiac signs and planets. There are also rulership manuals that act like dictionaries today.

Symbolic characters represent a content. Often they are compressed figurative representations, gestures or glyphs.

Symbol signs can represent simple facts, e. g. 'thumbs upward' for the contents: 'like', or very complex substance such as the glyph for an astrological symbol.

The planet Uranus is a possible representation of the astrological symbol ♅ in this perspective. Already in ancient times the so-called hermetic principle "as above, so below" was defined, indicating that you can read the situation of all facets of interpretation represented by this symbol from the physical position of Uranus in the solar system. Depending on the point of Uranus in its orbit, this means harmony, stress, activity, rest, etc. One of the millennium-long tasks of astrology was to determine the meanings of their positions for all planets. Such a meaning is called in astrology "time quality". (This is not a physical, but a philosophical concept, because the physical time does not have a quality.) All rulerships of an astrological symbol are subject of the same astrological time quality at the same time.

The current era is often called the information age. Actually, collecting information occupies a wide area. Public 'information collectors' like Google and Wikipedia obtain quasi-scientific authority. The issue of data protection and privacy affects many areas of life.

With all pride on the quantity of the collected and available data it is however not always remembered that information by itself hardly has any relevance. Only its adhering to humans, states, economic structure etc. determinates a value or worthlessness.

The difference between the information about a fact and its meaning can be demonstrated by the example "death of one's father". Some meanings of this fact can be

- loss of a friend,
- end to a tyranny,
- profit of a large inheritance,
- nothing at all (because the father left many years ago and no contact existed)
- and much else.

So, a piece of information can have very different meanings.

But a given meaning can also realize itself in different facts. The meaning of "your partnership will completely transform" can be concreted as

- separation,
- new beginning with the same partner,
- loss of the partner,
- new partner,
- etc.

Hence, it is not plainly possible to conclude from information the meaning and vice versa. However, for people – both in self-understanding and in social interaction – the meanings are of crucial importance. The determination of the time quality in form of astrological symbols, the core task of astrology, provides these meanings. In this respect Astrology acts as a system of meanings, in contrast to the information system.

To determine the quality of time, theoretically any facet of the symbol content can be used. Planets however are well suited because of their spacious, easily observable and predictable movements. Each planet is practically clock hand on an enormous 'solar system clock', from which the time quality can be read off. The task of astrologers is the interpretation of the determined conditions into concrete life circumstances.

When there is talk of celestial bodies, the term 'effect' usually is understood physically. This is contrary to common word usage, in which certainly is spoken of non-physical effects of words and deeds. But to avoid all criticism, modern Astrology has opted for an (analog) synchronicity, which in the model of a clock can be depicted. That corresponds to the common principle of correspondence of celestial events and earthly processes, that is in use since the Sumerian era.

A physical effect of the planets according to their changing positions in the solar system is not yet to be found (except gravity). There may be, however, a still unknown active principle that carries forward the non-causal

Only after more than 200 000 years all main planets of the solar system are at the same time in the same place again.

As a Horoscope drawing is a stylized map of the Solar system to a given time, there is no chart created in the last 5,000 years identical to another calculated for a different time.

A possible explanation for such correspond-ences is the "collective unconscious" postulated by C.G.Jung.

It is said to contain an archaic memory of human experience whose parts he called archetypes.

synchronicity. One might assume the possibility that the often postulated matches between planet names, the mythology of the original name-bearer and the astrological interpretation originate from the same source.

Authors of many introductions to astrology intentionally wanted to follow this theory, they have chosen the way to explain astrological symbols by the mythology of the deity, whose name refers to the symbol. Usually the Greek tradition is referred to in this context.

But by which archetypes are we really reached when we use Roman god names? Through a presentation of the original Italic, but already in ancient times by Greek myths alienated world of gods, their aspects are to be brought to light, and compared with the currently used astrological symbols. This may lead to supplements and new insights concerning astrological symbols.

This section is based in particular on the following literature, where further information can be found:

Goos, Hannelore, Lexikon der astrologischen Zuordnungen, Bd. 1-5, Norderstedt 2018-2019.

Schäfer, Thomas, Bildersprache Astrologie, Wettiswil (CH) 1991.

Stuckrad, Kocku von, Geschichte der Astrologie, Beck'sche Reihe, München 2007.

Mercury

Prehistory

The Sumerians called the innermost planet in our solar system **Gud.ud** (the Jumping) or **Kakkab Marduk** (Marduk messenger); in Mesopotamia, it was the star of the god Nabû or Nebo, city god of Borsippa.

He is considered to be the god of penmanship and an inventor of the cuneiform script; loam board and stylus are his attributes. As god of wisdom, it was up to him to note the life data of every human into a list and thus decide their lifetime. One more of his surnames is "Herald", in the sense that he brought the resolutions of the other gods to the humans. As "Lord of West Point", the sunset point, he also had the role of a companion from life to death. Though it was never denied that Nabû was a powerful god, over the centuries, he has been portrayed differently, depending on the dominant conditions.

The Chaldean god Nebo, from a statue in the British Museum.

Seba (en) Seth
Star of Seth

Mercury hieroglyph
Sebeg
New Empire
1550–1070 BC

Among the Egyptians, the innermost planet was first called Sebeg, the "Star of Seth". Only in Greco-Roman times, when the cultural exchange in the eastern Mediterranean was in full swing, first Thoth and Anubis, later Thoth alone became the god of this planet.

The different representations of Nabû and the Egyptian variability made it difficult for the Greek astronomer-philosophers to find a corresponding deity of their own pantheon for this celestial body. Both Apollo and Hermes were considered. Therefore, first the profane name "Sun companion" or "Stilbon" (Sparkling) was used. Later, however, Hermes prevailed generally. As part of the grecianisation of the Roman religion, the Roman god Mercury was equated him.

MERCURIUS as a Roman god

There were also attempts to derive 'MERCURIUS' from the name of an Etruscan gens *mercu.

But these remained speculation.

As shown in the history of the city of Rome, the earliest common place of the villages on the seven hills was a marketplace, the later FORUM BOARIUM (cattle market, s. p. 4). Because it was for strangers not allowed to enter Etruscan cities, the trade between Etruscans and neighbouring people from various ethnic groups was held at that place. Greek and Phoenician merchants also offered their goods at this market. A divine protector of the MERX (merchandise goods) can be assumed, and the god name MERCURIUS could be derived from this word.

Around the time of Rome's foundation a sort of bartering was practised in this market. Raw copper (AES RUDE) or weighted bronze ingots (AES SIGNATUM), labeled or pictured primarily by a flock, served as measures of value.

Until the 3rd century BC coins in central Italy were made uniquely from bronze, because this material was availiable there. The currency standard was called AS. All other coins were valuted in multiples or divisions of the AS. The first known Roman silver coin dates from 281 BC.

The Latin term for money PECUNIA derives from PECUS, the word for small cattle, which suggests that the first forms of money in Rome were goats and sheep. Around 278 BC the casting of bronze coins started with Mercury as coin image. These so-called AS-coins were later, decorated with Janus and Mercury, moved to the SEXTANS (= 1/6 AS).

Coin with Mercury

Despite the various speculations among the religious scholars in the past 200 years the original background of this deity is still unknown. It is unlikely that Mercury would have been brought to Rome by Greek merchants, for the Greeks of the cities of Greater Greece (the cities outside the motherland located around the Mediterranean) worshiped Hercules as protector of trade routes. A possible connection to the Etruscan god Thums is also mentioned in the literature, however without substantiation. Thus he seems to have been an Italian god, despite the late records of his cult.

After the city was formed, in 495 BC Mercury's main temple, located between the Palatine and the Aventine, became an inaugurated building. Coevally with its foundation a merchant guild was established, which was besides the organization of the temple service also responsible for the maintenance of the grain exchange.

Previously, the grain trade was exclusively in the hands of the patricians, who had repeatedly triggered famines by extortionate prices. By becoming connected to the temple of Mercury the corn stock exchange became a quasi-divine status, which terminated the stock market speculation possibilities. At the same time, the grain distribution to needy families was installed there.

The consecration of the temple was not as usual performed by a ruling patrician consul, but instead by a plebeian senator with an Etruscan name.

It is possible that the refusal of the service of a consul expressed the last resistance of the patricians against the regulation of the grain trade, which had been their source of income; they worshipped Hercules as the god of merchants instead of Mercury. The connection of Mercury with Ceres, the tutelary goddess of the plebeian community, suggests his relationship with the plebeians.

On the oldest cult calendars MERCURIUS is not yet shown. The first event where he is mentioned is the LECTISTERNIUM of 399 BC as a partner of Neptune. From 217 BC on he is recorded as counterpart of Ceres during the major public gods hostings and thus accepted in the circle of DII CONSENTES.

By incorporating Mercury into the circle of state gods, the enormous importance of commerce for Rome's existence was finally acknowledged.

Mythological remains

Concerning a Roman or Italian origin of Mercurius no evidence exists. The view is based only on literary records from the 2nd century BC onwards. These are possibly based on folktales, but such sources are not explicitly mentioned.

A very early connection between Mercury and Rome exists in literature, and is reported by Pausanias, Livy and Dionysius of Halicarnassus – although in different descriptions of details. Here a short compilation:

> Narration tells that Mercury and Carmenta had a son called Euander of Pallene. This divine offspring was born and raised up in Arcadia, an area of the Greek Peloponnese. As an adult Euander with a few faithful companians moved to Italy. At the place where later the city of Rome would arise, together with his small band he built a settlement. His mother Carmenta possibly joined him, because, according to Hyginus, she is said to have changed fifteen letters of the Greek Alphabet in such a way that her son would have introduced that as "Latin script" to the Latins. Euander called his settlement Pallantium after either his son or his Greek hometown. The place could have been on the Palatine, which should explain the hill's name. The myth also tells that Euander hospitalised Heracles, who, being exhausted, would have dwelled in Italy, after having robbed the cattle of the giant Geryon. Euander embodies in this myth the "good guy", who brings back the cattle to Heracles that previously was stolen by Vulkanus' son Cacus.
>
> Subsequently Euander is said to have built the cult place ARA MAXIMA for Hercules on the site of the later FORUM BOARIUM.

A LECTISTERNIUM (plural LECTISTERNIA) was a public hosting of deities, a Greek habit, introduced by the Sibillini Books (s. p. 43) : On an urban place, which was in use at the time as a place of worship, dining sofas (Lecta) were put, and on them statues of the state gods and goddesses were set in pairs. During several days on dining tables in front of these food offerings were placed. This large ritual was performed when the city suffered a dire threat.

In addition, on their holidays also the hosting of single deities and public hospitality of female deities took place, the latter called SELLISTERNIA (sing. SELLISTERNIUM). (Livy)

Carmenta was allegedly the Roman goddess of obstetrics and prophecy. Although nothing else is known about her, a FLAMEN, a state priest, was instituted for her.

Map of the Peloponnese in Antiquity with Pallantium, mythical home-town of Euander

Although Evander's son was killed in war before he had children, the Roman patrician family "Gens Fabia" trace their origin back to him.

This narrative is, like many others, an attempt to explain the emerging city of Rome as being Greek influenced from the outset. This can be concluded from the completely un-Roman representation of Mercury as a family father. Possibly, folktales of Italian origin are here mixed up. Although in later Roman literature the Greek god Hermes is declared the equivalent to Mercury, he does not occur in this story.

Being a Roman god, Mercury had anyhow little in common with Hermes. Since in the Roman religion Saturnus was responsible for the deceased (s. funeral rites p. 91), the importance as a guide of souls into the afterlife (psychopompos) is pointless to Mercury. And a function as a messenger of the gods is in the Roman conception likewise irrelevant because Roman deities were omnipresent. They showed their will in various omens, which were interpreted by the augurs, and not brought by a divine herald.

Instead, in Rome and its provinces, the focus was on Mercury's patronage for trade and traders, an area that plays a very subordinate role in the divine competences of Hermes. Only the tendency to dishonesty (see below) seems to be common to both.

As there are no mythological roots for Mercury apart from the retold legend, our search will focus now the actual practice of the cult of Mercury to find traces of his divinity.

Cult

MERCURIUS was one of the state gods, the DEI CONSENTES (s. p. 10). Contrary to custom, he had no high priest (FLAMEN), but instead the MERCATORUM COLLEGIUM and they organized his ritual on May 15.

On the same day the high priest of VOLCANUS (FLAMEN VOLCANALIS) celebrated a sacrifice to MAIA, an old Italic goddess of fertility (BONA DEA) and namesake of the month of May. These celebrations were not restricted to Rome; MERCURIUS and MAIA festivals had already been celebrated in Latium before their introduction in Rome.

The sacrificial animal of Mercury is especially the billy goat. The offering of a calf and a pig are also documented. Usually wine was served as a libation, and this characterizes a cult that was not anchored in a pastoral people, because these sacrificed milk.

The connection of the grain exchange to the Mercury temple was symbolized by sacrificing wheat ear bundles.

Rituals from the time of the pastoral people include usually milk as Libation. Only afterwards, when Etruscans and Sicilian Greeks had brought viticulture to Latium, wine was used.

Consecration of an altar for Mercury with a billy goat as sacrificial animal.

Ovid (43 BC–probably 17 AC) described in volume 5 (May) of his FASTI (Six Books of the Calendar) a special ritual held in Rome:

Where this fountain exactly was situated, is no longer determinable. However, in the Roman imperial era there were Mercury thermae at the Porta Capena; they may have been built at that place.	673	EST AQUA MERCURII PORTAE VICINA CAPENAE;	There's Mercury's fountain close to the Capene Gate:
		SI IUVAT EXPERTIS CREDERE, NUMEN HABET.	It's potent, if you believe those who've tried it.
	675	HUC VENIT INCINCTUS TUNICA MERCATOR ET URNA PURUS SUFFITA, QUAM FERAT, HAURIT AQUAM.	Here the merchant, cleansed, with his tunic girt, Draws water and carries it off, in a purified jar.
		UDA FIT HINC LAURUS, LAURO SPARGUNTUR AB UDA	With it he wets some laurel, sprinkles his goods
		OMNIA, QUAE DOMINOS SUNT HABITURA NOVOS;	With damp laurel: those soon to have new owners.
		SPARGIT ET IPSE SUOS LAURO RORANTE CAPILLOS	And he sprinkles his hair with dripping laurel too
	680	ET PERAGIT SOLITA FALLERE VOCE PRECES	And with that voice, that often deceives, utters prayers:
		"ABLUE PRAETERITI PERIURIA TEMPORIS," INQUIT	'Wash away all the lies of the past,' he says,
		"ABLUE PRAETERITAE PERFIDA VERBA DIE.	'Wash away all the perjured words of a day that's gone.
		SIVE EGO TE FECI TESTEM FALSOVE CITAVI	If I've called on you as witness, and falsely invoked
		NON AUDITURI NUMINA MAGNA LOVIS,	Jove's great power, hoping he wouldn't hear:
	685	SIVE DEUM PRUDENS ALIUM DIVAMVE FEFELLI,	If I've knowingly taken the names of gods and goddesses,
		ABSTULERINT CELERES IMPROBA VERBA NOTI,	In vain: let the swift southerlies steal my sinful words,
		ET PATEANT VENIENTE DIE PERIURIA NOBIS,	And leave the day clear for me, for further perjuries,
		NEC CURENT SUPERI SI QUA LOCUTUS ERO.	And let the gods above fail to notice I've uttered any.
		DA MODO LUCRA MIHI, DA FACTO GAUDIA LUCRO,	Just grant me my profit, give me joy of the profit I've made:
	690	ET FAC, UT EMPTORI VERBA DEDISSE IUVET."	And make sure I'll have the pleasure of cheating a buyer.'

TALIA MERCURIUS POSCEN- TEM RIDET AB ALTO, SE MEMOR ORTYGIAS SUR- RIPUISSE BOVES.	Mercury, on high, laughs aloud at such prayers, Remembering how he himself stole Apollo's cattle.

It is doubtful whether this text represents an actual cult. It is quite possible that the poem is just a product of Ovid 's poetry. In this text, written around the turn of the eras, the Roman Mercurius is equated with the Greek Hermes, which corresponds to the literary, but not to the religious customs. The most important ritual objects from this time, the still existing votive stones, do not show any relation to Hermes.

The content of the poem shows clear the arrogance of the patrician Ovid against the small traders. In addition, only the patrician merchants could afford slaves as their middlemen (making them safe from personal pursuit of fraud), while the retailers had to transact their business personally and thus could allow themselves much less deceits.

Here Ovids illustrates the prejudices of a patrician, who lives from his estate and pursues noble arts, towards the plebeian trader who has to work day in day out for his income. And, certainly, envy also plays a role in this, because traders were often richer than traditional patrician families.

Hence, it is entirely probable that Ovid's alleged prayer doesn't quote an original text at all, but solely was a product of his own creativity.

Mercury relief on a silver vase
Contrary to Hermes he carries
the messenger staff left,
but a purse right

Especially in Roman times, traders could not afford obvious trickeries, in no time that would have gotten around. In ancient times, when people were reliant on the offers of traveling traders, who on their regular sales tours always visited the same villages and towns, clear fraud would have been life-threatening. People did not shy away of getting physical when they were grossly defrauded. A Roman merchant, both in the city itself and in the provinces, relied on his reputation, and he could only preserve it if he was not 'enterprising' beyond the norm. Impudent theft of a whole herd of cattle, as it is attributed to the Greek Hermes, certainly does not belong to that.

"As usual among the Romans, immediately after the first settlements were built, trading posts were established. First of all this was probably organized for the necessary food supply, then everyday objects were delivered, in the end luxury goods followed, on which the Roman officers laid great emphasis." (GardenStone, Die Rückkehr der Göttin Nehalennia, p. 175).

This was all the more true in the provinces, where individually travelling merchants often always served the same routes. A fraud then could have had easily fatal consequences.

Mercury cult in the provinces

Merchants played an important role in the romanisation of the conquered territories. As far as they were Roman citizens, they were allowed to transport their goods on the road network built and maintained by the military. They could also obtain permission for the use of relay points and hostels. In cases of conflict, they were entitled to ask the army for help. If they were Roman citizens, they were allowed to refer to Roman law opposite to the local right. Therefore, especially in the provinces the acquisition of Roman citizenship was highly appreciated.

Since the army depended on traders in their supply organization, the merchants and their guilds had even greater importance in the provinces than in the city of Rome itself. In GardenStone's book quoted here these connections are clearly and comprehensively presented particularly on the long-distance trade with Britain.

Of course, the traders brought with them their trading god Mercury. But, as customary, by following the INTERPRETATIO ROMANA (s. p. 7), Mercury was identified with the gods invoked by their local business partners. By doing that the Romans assured themselves of the favour of these 'higher powers'; in return they usually offered a votive altar stone.

Most of such sacred stones were found in the provinces. And that documents the common religious 'business practice' by the hundreds: the respective deity was promised a votive altar if a particular trade or a mercantile expedition was finished profitable. For security reasons, both Mercury and the respective local deity were bestowed.

Once the expected success was achieved, the stone was commissioned with a corresponding dedication text. The closing formula that identifies these votive stones reads

V • S • L • M
VOTUM SOLVIT LIBENS MERITO
(He has fulfilled his vow, willingly, as it should.)

or a similar phrasing with the same meaning.

"Business men with identical profession or from the same town seem often to have formed a guild (COLLEGIUM or CORPUS). This is well-known e. g. from merchants (NEGOTIATORES CIVITATIS MATTIACORUM) in the German town now called Wiesbaden, they also had their own guild house (SCOLA). It is assumed that in every city of the Roman Rhineland similar guilds existed, either professionally or city bound. "
(GardenStone, Nehalennia, p. 167)..

On such stones found in the provinces the Roman Mercurius is often mentioned together with a local counterpart. A few examples are:

NAME	FOUND LOCATION	COMMENTARY
M. SUSURRIO	Aachen	probably Celtic, maybe Celtic-Germanic
M. TOUTENUS?	Bingen	Celtic
M. VASSOCALE(TI)S	Bitburg	probably Celtic
M. GEBRINIUS	Bonn	Celtic or Germanic-Celtic
M. CHANNINIUS	Rohr (D), Blankenheim (NL)	Germanic tribal god of the Cananefates
M. LEUD(ISIO) oder LEDUDISIANUS	Eschweiler-Lohn	
M. VISUCIUS	Esthal, Tholey-Wareswald	Gallo-Roman
M. CISSONIUS	Heddernheim, Rheinzabern	Originally Gallic or from Germanic neighbour tribes.
M. HRANNO	Bonn-Hemmerich	Germanic, Suebian?
M. ABGATIACUS?	Kleinich	Gallic or Gallo-Roman
M. ARVENORIX	Würzburg	Celtic-Germanic,
M. AVERNUS	Cologne, Krefeld and other places	The name is probably Celtic or adapted by Germanics from the Celtic language. Since all these votiv altars were found in areas where Germanic tribes lived, it could be a Germanic god.
M. CIMBRIANUS M. CIMBRIUS	Mainz, Heidelberg	Suebian?
M. ALAUNUS	Mannheim	Either Mediterranean or East-Germanic.
M. BIGENTIUS	Neumagen	Probably Gallo-Germanic
M. LOVANTUCARIS	Tholey-Wareswald	?
M. EXCINGIORIGIATIS	-	Celtic

Traders learned from foreign contacts usually about those deities of their trading partners, who were called by them in connection with business. Coincidentally, to writers such as Tacitus the merchants served as a source of information about distant lands, which had never been visited by them personally. So much misinformation becomes understandable.

NAME	FOUND LOCATION	COMMENTARY
M. GEBRINIUS	Bonn	Originally Gallic, then Gallo-Germanic.
M. NUNDINATOR	Wiesbaden	Could be Gallic or Gallo-Germanic, or Mercury himself (As protector of merchants).
M. MATUTINUS	Saarbrücken	Roman
M. SENO(TENSIS?)	-	Gallic or Gallo-Germanic
M. ERIAUSIUS ODER FRIAVSIUS?	Ubbergen (NL)	Germanic

(From: GardenStone, The Mercurius Wodan-Complex, pp.13, stripped-down)

Votiv stone for
MERCURIUS AVERNUS

Reports from traveling merchants have probably caused Tacitus to remark, that Mercury was the supreme god of the Germanic peoples.

In his book called "Germania" he wrote in the 9th section:

DEORUM MAXIME MERCURIUM COLLUNT, CUI CERTIS
DIEBUS HUMANIS QUOQUE HOSTIIS LITARE FAS HABENT.

Translated:
As for gods, Mercury is the one they worship most, and on certain days they think it right to propitiate him even with human victims.

J.B. Rives translation

(more to this in GardenStone: The Mercury-Wodan-Complex).

Mercury in Astrology

Mercury is commonly taken as the name of the innermost planet in our solar system. At the same time Mercury denotes the astrological symbol, whose status can be read from the astronomical orbit data of the celestial body. The angle of view to the symbol is accorded to the different astrological directions which describe it from different perspectives. Depending on whether the concern is more focused toward mental processes, character descriptions, or the determination of events, different aspects of the Mercury symbol attract attention.

Therefore, the following description may not be complete in every respect – the German "Lexikon der astrologischen Zuordnungen" (rulership book) contains more than 2 200 key words referring to this planet symbol.

Mercury is designated with the glyph ☿. According to the explanation of Gertrud Hürlimann the upper lying semicircle symbolizes the soul (as stylized moon), the middle circle the spirit (as a stylized sun) and the cross stands for matter (signum for the planet Earth). This formulaic pictogram of Mercury therefore contains the symbols for all three components of a personality and thus promises a possible integration of spirit, soul and matter. The soul is located at the highest point, above spirit and matter as a basis, but the rootedness in the material becomes clear also.

In modern western astrology, Mercury symbolizes active thinking and acting. It is thereby one of the ambassadors of a person's essence, which cannot articulate itself. Without being aware, in speech and action we send information about our real nature and just as automatically we take such information from all people we are concerned with.

In the German language we see the impact of the Mercury symbol:
The word *handeln* has the double meaning of 'to buy and sell' and 'to do something actively'.

Mercury's position in the horoscope therefore shows in which way we interact with our environment. In concrete terms the astrological Mercury symbol stands for

- learning to speak in early childhood,
- reading and writing, up to literary activity,
- exchange of ideas and discussion, and in addition the necessary intellectual abilities for that
- interest in knowledge generally.

In this way the essence of a person shows up.

Particularly good success of the 'ambassador activity' of Mercury is displayed if he is positioned in the same zodiac sign as the sun, which symbolizes the person's essence. Is Mercury placed in neighbouring signs, the sun and its ambassador act in different ways and the affected people regularly experience, that what they say or how they act does not arrive as intended in their environment.

> By thinking, speaking and acting, the innermost essence of a person becomes recognizable.

But the Mercury symbol does not simply contain a unilateral mediating role, the ability to take the experience of others and incorporate into own actions is displayed too. Astronomically, the reflected light from the planet Mercury is so weak that it seems to disappear in the telescope when it comes closer than 8 degrees of radian to the sun. This position is called from time immemorial "burned" (combustion). People with this constellation in the horoscope often don't have the ability to integrate experiences of others. They have to try everything themselves even at the risk of failure. Especially in this negative form it is distinctly evident which skills are expressed by the Mercury symbol.

Another special position is called "Cazimi", an Arab term for a planet located within 17 arcminutes from the sun, literally 'in the heart of the sun'. Surely only the sun is recognizable in this case, because it over-radiates the respective planet. With Mercury this position can be interpreted as particularly positive.

"Here a comparison in order to differentiate Cazimi from combustion:
When a guest or petitioner visits the court of the king (sun), then he will have to subordinate himself deeply, and perform many gestures of modesty. He cannot act any more as he wishes, but has to be subordinate, even hide himself. This means combustion.

But if the guest receives an audience by the king himself, and then stands directly before the throne in the throne room, then his position is suddenly greatly strengthened, and the king grants him his request or desires. This position provides privileges and advantages, and sometimes even prosperity. "

(http://wiki.astro.com/astrowiki/de/Cazimi)

A key area for the astrological symbol Mercury is exchange, exchange not only of words but of things, goods, merchandise. This means the activity of selling, buying and trading. The position of this planet is important for all types of mercantile activities and sales contracts, not only in a natal chart, but also at the moment the contract is concluded (mundane). Astrologically experienced merchants do not only observe strong or weak positions, but especially the so-called retrograde motion.

The orbital period of the Earth around the Sun is one year, but that of Mercury only 88 days. When watching Mercury daily through a telescope, it seems to run backwards intermittently. This optical phenomenon is caused by the different orbital periods and is called traditionally **retrograde**. Basically, the phenomenon is to be observed on all planets, but because of the large difference in Mercury's orbital period this is in particular striking here.

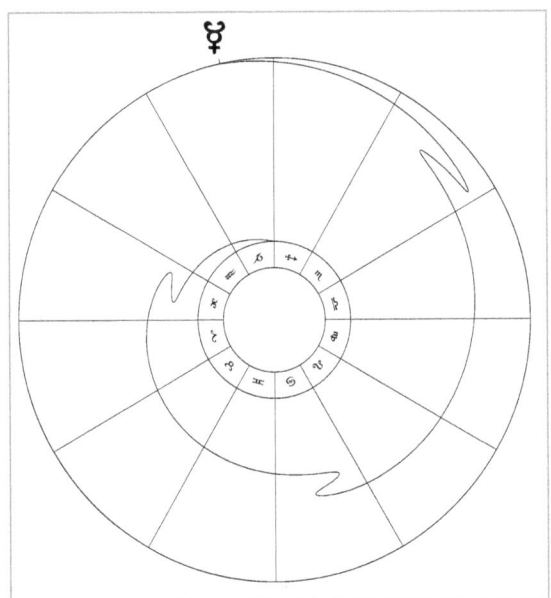

The course of Mercury in the zodiac 2013 –
clearly visibly the apparent backward motion.
(created by Astro Plus)

If possible, in times of a retrograde Mercury no new contracts should be concluded because their fulfilment often becomes difficult.

Starting of a company or a transaction during such a period is also not favourable. It is more of a time in which things that had already been started can be brought to a successful conclusion. Especially operations and transactions that started with difficulties and had been set aside can now be resumed and with good chances of success brought to conclusion. The consolidation of existing businesses are particularly favoured.

The end of the retrograde period is not reached when Mercury optically runs forward again but when it gets back to the point where it had entered the apparent retrograde motion.

These rules are often observed; the astrologer M. M. Herm, who had lived in the United States for a long time, reported that there are pocket calenders for merchants and bankers published for decades in which the regressiveness data of Mercury is noted. And the German astrology mail-order shop "Astronova" annually provides clients with a regressiveness overview of Mercury.

Summary

Regarding the planetary symbol Mercury as seen in modern Western Astrology, the central points are linguistic communication – reported already in the mythology of 'Mercurius' son' Euander – and all types of commercial activity which are to be found in relation to the sphere of influence of the Roman god MERCURIUS.

The specific tasks of the Greek god Hermes as agent of the gods does not occur because the Roman deities were permanently omnipresent. A special messenger was not needed, every god could be invoked everywhere, especially in his temple. The role of the leader to the underworld is attributed nowadays, if at all, to Pluto. The art of healing is more often ruled by Chiron. The Greek Hermes is therefore in the planet Symbol Mercury actually no longer present.

Regarding cheating, stealing and deceiving, the general attitude can be observed that merchants basically seek their own advantage and do not really dislike trickery and deception. Yet, the desire to achieve profit is not a flaw in the character, but necessary to maintain the business, which also has an important function in providing people with the goods of daily needs. However, bigger scams are not part of Mercury's sphere.

Thus, in today's astrology only minor thefts are regarded under the sign of Mercury, robbery belongs to Mars and all kinds of deception and fraud to Neptune. Here too, a shift of meaning into the direction of the Roman conceptions can be found.

Overall, one can therefore conclude that in today's Western Astrology the Mercury symbol largely contains meanings corresponding to the Roman tradition of MERCURIUS and only very few depicted by the Greek Hermes.

Allegorical figure of Mercury
on the
Puppenbrücke (Doll's Bridge)
in Lübeck from 18. century

Some rulerships of the planet symbol
Mercury as facet model

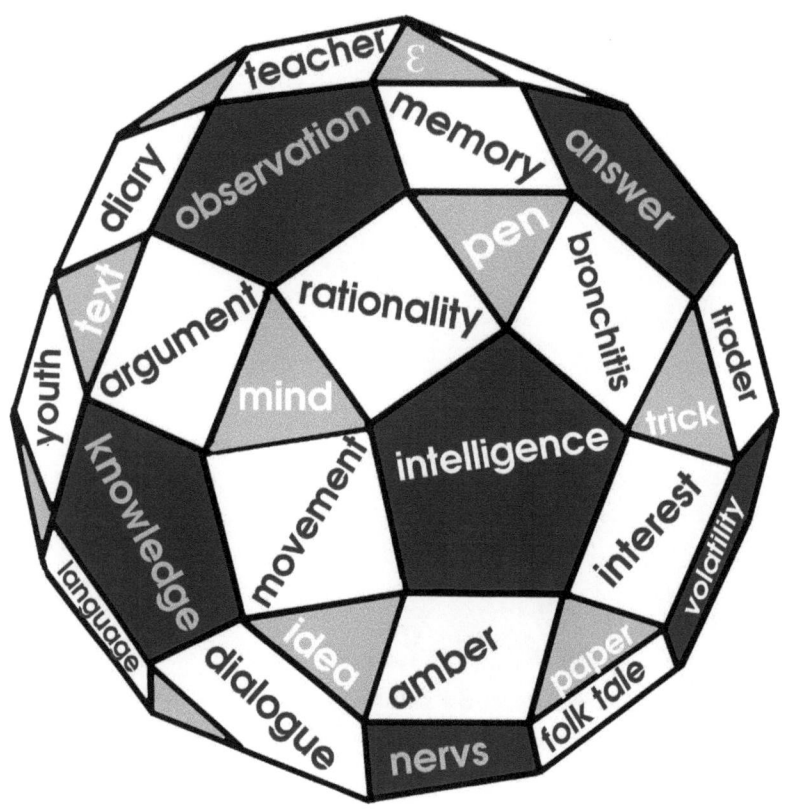

Besides the mentioned titles this section is based in particular on the following literature, where further information can be found:

Translated by A. S. Kline (Übers. u. Hrsg.), Ovid Metamorphoses,
http://www.poetryintranslation.com/PITBR/Latin/OvidFastiBkFive.htm

Hürlimann, Gertrud I., Astrologie, Zürich 1987.

Muth, Robert, Einführung in die griechische und römische Religion,
2. Auflage, Darmstadt 1998.

Venus

Prehistory

At first for the early observers the second planet of our solar system caused a problem: In sky observations it appears both as morning and as evening star. To various people from past times it was not clear that it concerns the same celestial body.

In poetry and in diverse mythological notations the difference between morning and evening star still remained.

A separate treatment can even be found in astrological literature of the 20th century (see below).

Ishtar-Relief, 2nd Millenium BC

The Sumerians recognized both manifestations as the same planet. This is evidenced by the Venus tablets of Ammi−saduqa, the oldest preserved and known written document with planetary observations. The star was called Dibalt, and its ruler was Inanna (Ishtar Ishhara, Irnini), city goddess of Uruk. She served as a goddess of love, but also as a warrior, her sacred animal was the lion. The Ishtar Gate from Babylon (Pergamon Museum in Berlin) suggests that this goddess played an important role for the capital too.

She was worshipped as the embodiment of female sexuality, as described already in some cuneiform documents and subsequently with different names around the Mediterranean.

The Egyptians saw in the morning and the evening star two celestial bodies. They were classified as being masculine, the evening star was called "sky-crosser", the morning star "morning god".

The Greek astronomers initially distinguished a morning star named Phosphoros (lightbringer), Eosphoros (bringer of dawn) or Proinos (the early morning) and an evening star Hesperus (named after the titan Hesperos). According to Pliny the Elder, Pythagoras is said to have discovered again that these names indicate the same planet. In the context of the cultural exchanges between Greeks, Egyptians and Babylonians, Greek philosophers started to deal with astrology, whereby they identified their Aphrodite with the aforementioned oriental love goddess. Her Sumerian function as a warrior was no longer taken into account.

As then the denominations of planetary symbols were tranferred to Roman deities, a goddess Venus was chosen for this planet.

It is striking that in all ancient pantheons the deity responsible for this planet occupies an outsider position; in several way it is tried to integrate her:

Hieroglyphs for the planet Venus,

first line
the evening star
with the night bark,

below
the morning Star

- In Mesopotamia Innana had immigrated from the mythical site Aratta outside the Sumerian countries and was considered as a daughter of the sky god An or as a daughter of the moon god Nanna and the moon goddess Ningal.
- In Egypt the planet is assigned to two gods who are otherwise not anchored in mythology.
- Aphrodite in Greece appears in the age of the olympic gods in Cyprus and is received by them as coequal. There are several reinterpretation attempts toward an inclusion into the family of Greek gods.

The Roman Venus is a foreigner too, as shown in the following.

VENUS as a Roman goddess

It is unclear where the name Venus comes from. Related literature offers a derivation from the Indo-European root word *uen- (1), *$uenə$-. which means 'strive for, wish, love, achieve, win, triumph', and a second derivation from the linguistic roots of 'wine' (lat. VINUM) and 'poison' (lat. VENENUM). Particularly to the authors of the 19th century, the connection of the goddess with (sexual) lust aroused rather ambivalent feelings which accordingly led to corresponding interpretations. In any case, "VENUS" in Latin grammar is not a noun but an attributive adjective. Before Christ there is no mention of Venus without a characterising noun.

The first wine commonly was sacrificed to IUPPITER and VENUS CAELESTIS. Cato reports in his ORIGINES, that the Etruscan King Mezentius of Caere had humiliated the subjected Latins this way, that he claimed the first fruits of field and vineyard for himself (approximately in the 6th century BC)

In Rome, Venus has established herself as a deity relatively late. As early as 283 BC a temple (for VENUS FELIX or VENUS OBSEQUENS) was built on the Esquiline, which was done primarily for political reasons. At that time Rome sought supremacy over Lazio. VENUS CAELESTIS and IUPPITER were the highest deities of the Latin League, to which Rome belonged (s. p. 5). By erecting this temple, the Venus sanctuaries in the Latin cities of Ardea and Lavinium became secondary, and the central importance of Rome for the area was demonstrated. The fact that building this temple was not payed by a patrician sponsor as usual, but by the fines of unfaithful wives and that no state priest (FLAMEN) was appointed, shows clearly, that this did not concern a religious act.

The cult stone in this temple was labelled VENUS FELIX. The other epithet OBSEQUENS (submissive) was added later, based on the assumption that the victory over the Samnites was her decisive contribution in response to the vowed selfsacrifice of the military commander, the consul PUBLIUS DECIUS MUS. Thus, the goddess had virtually acknowledged the request of the Romans by accepting the offer.

After the Romans were in 217 BC in the Second Punic War defeated devastatingly at the Battle of Lake Trasimeno, the Sybillini Books were consulted. That oracle recommended to rob the Carthaginian (Phoenician) goddess Tanit and bring her from her temple on Sicily to Rome. The Romans followed the advice by occupying the shrine at mount Eryx and then moved the image of the goddess to the temple of VENUS VERTICORDIA on the Roman Capitol Hill and called her VENUS ERYCINA.

The 'alluring' of hostile deities in the form of moving their cult images, and thereby getting an advantage in a battle, was a method that Rome had already successfully used in various smaller wars. Livy reports that during the struggle for the city of Veii a Roman temple was promised to the town goddess. After Rome's victory it was build by Camillus and consecrated to the former goddess of Veii (Temple of IUNO REGINA).

Venus (maybe in copying other Italian town's habit the tutelary goddess of Rome whose name was forbidden to be named) was to this time already part of the circle of the twelve state gods; from 217 BC on her statue was placed next to that of Mars in LECTISTERNIA (s. p. 27). This step towards the establishment of an institutionalized Venus cult may also have been political: Romans sought a divine blessing in defending against the Carthaginians under Hannibal, in the end successfully winning in 201 BC.

The Sibillini Books were a collection of oracles written in Greek Hexameters, allegedly by a fortune teller from the area of Naples (Sybille of Cumae).

In times of distress, they were consulted by specially appointed dignitaries, the DECEMVIRI SACRIS FACUNDIS, with the question, which religious measures would be necessary to reconcile the gods and to avert the disaster. Only the interpretation was released, the underlying sentence remained secret; thus, the interpreters had a completely free hand for their own ideas.

Altar of the twelve gods, use unknown:
maybe the brink of a well or an zodiac altar,
marble, found in Gabii (Italy), 1st century AC

Gnaeus Naevius (265 – 201 BC) wrote comedies and tragedies in Greek style combined with national Roman materials.

In the epic BELLUM PUNICUM the Roman myth of the exodus of the Aeneads from Troy to Rome's founding is inserted. (Books 1 and 2).

Quintus Ennius (* 239 – 169 BC) was a writer, whose main importance consisted in the transfer of Greek literature into Latin. His ANNALES, an epic poem in 18 books, covers Roman history from the fall of Troy to the year 184 BC. They were the main source for Virgil's AENAEIS. Both writers translated the name Aphrodite with Venus.

In the 1st pre-Christian century several works were published, which described the mythical origin of Rome. The most important ones:

Publius Vergilius Maro (70 – 19 BC) AENAEIS

Dionysios of Halikarnassos (54 BC – 8 AD) ANTIQUITATES

Titus Livius (59 BC – 17 AD) AB URBE CONDITA

However, the adaptation of the Greek-Phoenician cult on Sicily was not possible in its original form. At its regular place on Mount Eryx temple prostitution was part of it, and this would have been inacceptable on the 'respectable' Capitol Hill. Therefore in 184 BC outside the city in front of the Porta Collina another temple for VENUS SALACIA was built. This became the temple for 'fallen girls' and registered prostitutes.

And the third step to get Venus established as an important goddess in the Roman pantheon was also based on reasons of state. Caesar and Augustus interpreted her as a "Roman Aphrodite" for the legitimacy of their, not undisputed, rule as dictators/emperors. In addition they declared a mythical story described several times by poets regarding the (proven wrong) founding myth of the city as 'truth':

According to Greek tradition, Aphrodite was the mother of Aeneas; after the fall of Troy he ended up in Italy and his descendants founded Rome. His son Ascanius, also called Julus, was the ancestor and eponym of the gens Julia, to which Caesar and Augustus belonged. (condensed summary by Hannelore Goos)

That way these emperors justified their divine origin which in turn legitimized their claim to power. To represent this visually, they built the so-called Forum of Caesar, first Imperial Forum in Rome, with the Temple of VENUS GENETRIX (ancestress), consecrated in 46 BC. However, no state priest, but a collegium was established for it.

Finally, in 121 AD emperor Hadrian started erecting the largest temple building in the history of the city of Rome, the double temple of Venus and Roma, the latter was a divine personalizing of the city. With the really unusual monumental building, Hadrian, highly controversial as ruler, wanted to show himself in the succession of Romulus. For the first time Venus appears here without an epithet. The combination of Venus and Roma makes it quite probable that this temple belongs to the city goddess of Rome whose real name

Column row of the Hadrian double Temple for Venus and Roma

had to be kept secret under penalty of death, in order to prevent enticing her away by enemies, as described above.

Like the predecessors the Roman Venus is thus also a deity who is not anchored in the original religion, but came from outside. Once becoming a Roman Venus, her political instrumentalization is obvious.

Mythological remains

Initially, the Latin word VENUS did not refer not to an entity or a person, but was a possible virtue of a deity, such as divine mercy or divine benevolence. Therefore, up to 2nd century AD the term VENUS was used as a epithet. Expressions such as VENUS IOVIA (Jupiter mercy) or VENUS KERRIA (benevolence of Ceres) indicate that in early Roman times no independent fertility and vegetation goddess called "Venus" existed, but the venus attribute could be added to each deity.

The Osci, an early Italic people worshipped a goddess **herentas** also under the name VENUS HERENTAS. Their cult is said to have been taken over by the Latins in the form of fertility rituals in the month of April, when the earth opens again (APERIRE = to open). A corresponding female deity was worshiped in Lavinium as VENUS FRUTIS in a temple called FRUTINAL.

Another goddess in this series is VENUS FISICA, tutelary deity of treaties and city goddess of Pompeii. Her cult image in a long tunic, with cloak, tiara and scepter makes the difference to the Greek Aphrodite clear. Already since the early 2nd century BC the original meaning of the (from Greek derived) name FISICA

VENUS FISICA

was no longer known; LUCIUS CORNELIUS SULLA (138–78 BC) used it in the sense of "queen of heaven, earth and sea".

So the Romans obviously have applied the term VENUS to several female deities.

In the ostentatious "meals offered to gods" (LECTISTERNIA, s. p. 27), a Venus idol was placed next to Mars on a recliner. A connection between the two deities is represented by Cupido between them, suggesting a legal relationship unequal to the Aphrodite myth.

Until the time of the empire statues of Roman deities usually were made by Etruscan sculptors, and thus, the great similarity of the Venus image to the Etruscan goddess Turan is not surprising.

Venus was the epithet of a number of goddesses who in literature were merged into one deity with that name:

Etruscan bronze:
Turan
(about 550-450 BC)

The Latin verb VENERARE=to worship derives from the same root as VENUS (English: venerate).

The Greek educated poets and writers in Rome interpreted Aphrodite as Venus. However, that stayed literary only, it never became a religious cult.

Christan writers of the Middle Ages often used "Venus" as a synonym for female debauchment without considering a religious background..

Among others Virgil mythologized Venus as the ancestress of the Romans, caring mother of the ancestor Aeneas.

In this context, he tells how she cajoled a suit of armor from Vulcano for her son Aeneas. The blacksmith god is not her husband here, as it would have been equal to the Greek couple Aphrodite-Hephaestus: In Virgil's epic the nymph Charis is Vulcano's housewife.

Christian writers
such as Augustinus,
depicting heathen
religion, were not inter-
ested in differentiating
information.

Unfortunately they are
often the only source of
knowledge concerning
Roman deities.

About
VENUS CLOACINA:
Pliny tells the following
legend: Her shrine was
donated by Romulus and
Tarquin, after the two
had purified themselves
at this point with myrtle
twigs to start peace
negotiations between
Romans and Sabines.

VENUS LIBERTINA was
probably by a linguistic
shifting equated with the
ancient Italian goddess of
the dead LIBITINA and
so became patroness of
undertakers and
funeral services.

The old view was, that VENUS was the name in VENUS HERENTAS, VENUS FRUTIS, etc. together with an epithet. In this book those current scholars are followed, who exactly see the opposite. Other examples are:

VENUS CAELESTIS: The divine benevolent to heaven belonging one.
From the 5nd century BC on used for the highest heavenly goddess, sometimes worshipped together with Jupiter, especially by the Latins.

VENUS CALVA: The divine benevolent bald-headed one
Probably an old Italian goddess to whom women sacrificed their hair in times of need, perhaps in order to make bows.

VENUS CLOACINA: The divine benevolent purifying one
Etruscan goddess of water, who had a shrine at the entrance of the main drainage channel (a former watercourse).

VENUS ERYCINA: The divine benevolent originating from Mount Eryx.
Imported from Sicily, probably the Phoenician Tanith.

VENUS FRUTIS: The divine benevolent budding one.
Worshipped in a temple called FRUTINAL in the Latin town of Lavinium.

VENUS FELIX: The divine benevolent good luck bringing one.
Name found on her cult stones on the Esquiline and in the temple built by Hadrian.

VENUS GENETRIX: The divine benevolent ancestress
Goddess of motherhood and domesticity with a feast day on September 26th; after Virgil the mythical progenetrix of the Roman people.

VENUS KALLIPYGOS: The divine benevolent beauty giving one.
Venerated in the Greek city of Syracusa.

VENUS LIBERTINA: The divine benevolent freeing one.
May be a mixing of VENUS ERYCINA with the plebeian goddess LIBERA.

VENUS MURCIA: The divine benevolent goddess of Aventine Hill.
MURCUS is said to have been an old name for the Aventine Hill; the word later in popular etymology moved to MURCIA (myrtle).

VENUS OBSEQUENS: The divine benevolent compliant one.
The goddess to whom consul PUBLIUS DECIUS MUSIUS promised his life in turn for the victory over the Samnites.

VENUS SALACIA: The divine benevolent patroness of sea water
Goddess of sea-salt and prostitutes.

VENUS VERTICORDIA: The divine benevolent turner of hearts.
Worshipped by patrician Matronae. She should turn the hearts of young girls to the husbands chosen by their fathers, and to morality.

VENUS VICTRIX: The divine benevolent victorious one
With that title the goddess VICTORIA was meant. She was honoured on October 9th together with the GENIUS PUBLICUS and FAUSTA FELICITAS on Capitol Hill.

From this list it becomes clear that the expression "VENUS" is merely a title or invocation formula. A goddess or a numen called Venus appears to have never existed in ancient Rome. Writers educated in Greek traditions translated "Aphrodite" into "Venus". What goddess was meant thereby, remains unclear. Even in later centuries beautiful female deities were called "Venus", without referring to a specific deity.

Venus as a generic designation has been kept until today. A famous example is the term "Venus figurines" for female statuettes from the neolithic period, the most famous being the Venus from Willendorf.

Cult

Cults of goddesses with the epithet Venus are reported from various towns in Latium. Such temples have stood in Ardea, Lavinium, Alba Longa and Gabii. Nothing is known about the nature of the service. Only after the cities had joined forces in the Latin League, VENUS CAELESTIS and Jupiter are mentioned as the patrons of their annual gatherings. While the god as IUPPITER LATIARIS (Jupiter of the Latins) was responsible for justice and legality, the goddess had the task of ensuring harmony and a peaceful mood.

Since the 3rd century BC she was also worshipped in Rome. Hence some details are known from the calendar.

On April 1st, the **VENERALIA** were celebrated, the festival of VENUS VERTICORDIA (Turneress of hearts, insofar as she prevents girls from immorality). This celebration combines older and newer elements. While the consumption of milk indicates that it derives from the peasants and herdsmen times in the Roman area (later wine was standard), the centering around a Venus statue shows later Etruscan or Greek influence, because images are unusual in the original Roman religion.

At this festival the married women (MATRO-NAE) went to the Venus temple, took off all jewel-lery and attached votive offerings from the statue and washed it thoroughly. Then they went to the temple of FORTUNA VIRILIS, which contained a warm spring with a bathhouse usually reserved for men only. There, the women undressed, crowned themselves with myrtle, drank milk with poppy seeds and honey and purified themselves by a bath. Dressed again they went back to the temple of Venus and adorned the now dried statue again with her golden chain, fresh flowers and other ornaments.

The back and forth is explained in the way that the statue of the chaste Venus initially stood in the temple

Venus figure in the style of Praxiteles, c. 50 BC.

The celebrations of the Roman calendar are listed in the books of Ovid called FASTI, poetry in the tradition of Greek didactic poems. Each month corresponds to a book, but only the first six remained. In addition to the data, customs and traditions are presented for each feast.

of FORTUNA VIRILIS, but was confronted there with all sorts of fornication, so that in 114 BC. she got a temple of her own.

In the years of the late Republic and the Empire the VINALIA APRILIS became more and more a pure wine festival with high alcohol consumption; the part of Jupiter worship disappeared..

On April 23, the **VINALIA URBANA** took place. In this first wine festival of the year the new wine was celebrated. The festival was dedicated to both, IUPPITER and VENUS CAELESTIS. The Jupiter ritual was held by his high priest and served the dedication of the sacral wine and the request for good weather for the new harvest. The Venus celebrations consisted of solemn tastings of the new profane wine made of the grapes pressed in the previous autumn.

Fragment of the Fasti Praenestini with the entry Vinalia (VIN)

In both cases, large amounts of wine were poured into a spillway between the temples of the two deities as offerings.

At the same time the festival of VENUS ERYCINA ET MERETRICUM took place; ordinary girls (PUELLAE VULGARES) and registered prostitutes (MERETRICES) gathered in the temple outside the PORTA COLLINA. They sacrificed myrtle (cleaning) and hedge mustard (remedy) and adorned the image of the goddess with rosaries. In return, they asked for beauty, attractiveness and wealthy punters.

On August 19th, the 'consecration birthday' of the Temple of VENUS OBSEQUENS was celebrated. This was the oldest Venus temple. It was also the day of VINALIA RUSTICA, the ceremonial opening of the vintage. Like at the spring wine festival also copious quantities of wine were poured out as a sacrifice. As an agricultural holiday, this day was also celebrated by gardeners, greengrocers and flower cultivators in honour of VENUS FRUTIS.

The information in older literature that Venus was an italic goddess of gardens and spring, who had been worshipped by crop and vine farmers in this respect is not altogether wrong, because quite a devotion existed to VENUS KERRIAE (merciful goddess of grain) and VENUS FRUTIS (gracious goddess of burgeoning).

Both the many names and the cult practice show that "Venus" originally was not an independent goddess, not a discreet entity, but rather an attitude of benevolence that was not attributed to female deities only. In contrast is the understanding of poets and Greek educated intellectuals who saw in Venus a mere translation of the word Aphrodite. This Greek view is still widely spread in current history and European astrology.

Venus in Astrology

We take for granted that Venus is the name of the second planet in our solar system. Additionally, in today's astrology Venus indicates a symbolic content, according to CG Jung's theory of archetypes, psychic complexes in the subconscious mind of all human beings. Linguistically, this expresses itself in the fact that the denomination *Venus* can be seen as a generic term.

At a closer look, however, we find astrology still presenting an evening and a morning star, which is expressed in the way that Venus 'reigns' in two zodiac signs, Taurus (morning star) and Libra (evening star). The rulerships can be easily divided into two groups (s. the model-like representations as facets diagrams on page 53 and page 54).

Some astrological authors, such as B. A. Mertz, decided to distinguish the two. Mertz defined that in an astrological chart Venus is interpreted as morning star (Taurus Venus), when the planet is placed before the sun clockwise and as evening star (Libra Venus), behind the central light. Since for astronomical reasons Venus can never depart more than 48° from the sun, this positioning is always clear. Mertz assigned the keyword "female sensibility" to the symbol of Venus, and differentiated between "reality based sensibility" (Taurus Venus) and "connective sensibility" (Libra Venus).

In the second half of the last century, there were several attempts to resolve the double rulership of Venus over two zodiac signs:

- **Edith Wangemann** postulated the hypothetical Transpluto, whom she called *ISIS* as the ruler of Libra. This celestial body had been calculated by the University of Paris, due to track fluctuations of Neptune. Because of the recent exploration of the Kuiper belt, where such a planet was not found, this assumption has become obscure.

- The Swiss astrologer **Hans Jörg Walter** postulated (the dwarf planet) *Ceres* as ruler of Taurus. Although his arguments seem quite valid, hardly any other astrologer followed him.

There may be a parallel between these movements and the research results in respect of the Roman goddess Venus: as in Roman religion no specific goddess can be found, but *Venus* stands as a principle of divine attitude, the astrological symbol of Venus could also characterize an attitude, which is reflected in the movements of several celestial bodies.

Within the different schools of astrology the divergent symbolic content is not always taken into account. Depending on whether the interpretation of the astrological symbols is more focused on mental processes, character

Bernd Arnulf Mertz

(* July 10th, 1924 in Berlin; † November 17th, 1996 in Frankfurt am Main, Germany), was a German actor, director, scenario writer and astrologer.

He wrote more than 25 books and ran an astrologers school in Frankfurt am Main in the 80s and 90s of the last century (together with his wife Christiane Eisler).

Edith Wangeman

*August 8th, 1917 in Magdeburg, Germany; † September 19th, 2000. The astrologer conducted the "Kosmobiosophic Society" founded by her husband to a significant movement within the German astrological scene and was editor of the magazine "Sein und Werden" (To be and to become).

Hans Jörg Walter

(born June 2nd, 1925) authored a number of astrological books. Both in his major work "Entschlüsselte Aspektfiguren" (Decoded Aspect Figures) as well as in a book about Chiron, he considers that the astrological ruler of the sign Taurus is the 1801 discovered asteroid Ceres.

descriptions or identification of events, the differences are considered more or less distinct. Some authors are quite aware of this, like Thomas Schäfer, who describes in his book "Bildersprache Astrologie" (Astrology as talking pictures) merely only Venus as the evening star. The lack of distinction found in the vast majority of astrologers means that the more than 2,200 keywords in the "Lexikon der astrologischen Zuordnungen" (German Rulership Book) refer to both forms of the planet symbol.

Nevertheless, there is an overarching principle regardless of different directions of astrology. Venus is designated with the glyph ♀. The circle represents the sun (mind) and the cross the earth (matter). Even the astrological symbol is part of the Venus symbol; in abstract form the Venus sign signalizes the primacy of mind over matter.

Like Mercury, the Venus symbol also signifies a messenger from a person's essence in an astrological chart, but in non-rational form, via emotions.

> By emotional expression it is mirrored how someone undergoes and appreciates himself and his opposite

When humans, in their innermost being, are in accord with themselves and the people around them, they radiate harmony. Differences cause disharmony.

Through the emotions that we show, we make it clear
- what value we assign to ourselves and the things belonging to us (morning star, Taurus principle),
- how we see other people and want to be seen by them (evening star, Libra principle).

The position of Venus in the chart shows wether we feel in innermost harmony with ourselves and our surrounding partners, and the points with lack of appreciation evoke negative emotions.

In concrete terms, the astrological Venus symbol stands

⇨ as **morning star** for:
- appreciation of the own person,
- joy about valuable possessions,
- harmonious embedding in natural processes,
- pleasure in enjoyment.

⇨ as **evening star** for:
- appreciation of partners in all relationships,
- joy of self-representation to the partners,
- demonstration of beauty,
- pleasure in sophistication.

In both cases, sexuality is included as a quasi natural element of these functions. The perception that sex is often stated in the foreground as a particular signature of the Venus symbol in astrological tradition, may on the one hand be caused by the fact that sexuality in the Christian-Jewish culture for centuries was greatly suppressed and thus represented something special. On the other hand this may also be accounted to the effort of astrologers, to find definitively something in common for evening and morning star, because, indeed, there is always only one of these two is present in the chart.

As described above, there were different reactions to this dilemma. which is still unsolved.

The Roman Venus deities were brought relatively late into the city of Rome. Here, the previous described picture of a goddess coming from outside into a pantheon is repeated. Symbolically, this points to the Libra-Venus, because the zodiac sign Libra generally stands for involvement with people and things that come from the outside and to which one must develop a positive or negative attitude.

Summary

Regarding the planet symbol Venus, as seen in modern western Astrology, it prioritises on the one hand appreciation of oneself and on the other hand the appreciation of partners. Both were united in the Greek Aphrodite myth as one character (even though current descriptions are often strongly distorted by the morality of the respective authors).

In Roman religion, however, already the falling apart of the two symbols morning and evening star are noticed, respectively Taurus Venus and Libra Venus.

Understanding of womanly self-esteem is indicated in the Roman rites of the VENERALIA. In the male-dominated world of Antiquity women's services generally respected the female threads of marriage, pregnancy and childbirth. A festival focused only at own joy and pleasure was certainly something unusual. This social view, however, has changed dramatically.

In today's Western cultures independence and a healthy self-esteem is expected from women. No woman has to put up with social contempt anymore, if she's looking for a lover herself. Most marriages are formally entered into 'forever', but in reality divorces cause no scandals. In this respect, many special aspects of the Venus symbol highlighted formerly are now standard practices and require no goddess for their legitimacy.

Venus is present at different places of ancient Rome as a symbol of relations, with an emphasis on social adjustment (VERTICORDIA) as well as on sexuality (SALACIA). Nowadays an important aspect of Venus forms the mediating function, as narrated from Pompeian VENUS FISICA.

In Rome, already in the late republic phase, the need to assign a religious symbol to the position of mediation and compensation can be observed. In the present, the skills related to harmonization play an important role in the world of work as well as in private life. This corresponds obviously to Venus evening star. The experienced astrologer can read the relevant skills or weaknesses of the native from the position of this Venus in his chart. If there are problems in this particular field, the horoscope shows solutions as well.

For the morning star, the references to values, in particular material ones are clear. Contrary to the conditions in the ancient world with land ownership as the most important property, nowadays money and goods, the possession of objects is dealt with up to collecting mania. This can manifestate itself in a negative form as compulsive hoarding. Overeating also belongs to the complex of this symbol. The corresponding attitudes are displayed depending on the positive or negative position of this Venus in the chart.

Attitudes to sexuality in its strict sense are nowadays symbolized by Pluto after its discovery. The emotional expression of physical well-being, represented as a result of physical self-esteem in this area, is of course included in the Venus symbol.

Roman Venus made of clay
ca. 1. – 3. cent. BC
ca. 6,5 cm high

Overall, it is clear that the development of social conditions, in particular the views on sexuality, heavily altered the view of modern Western Astrology at the symbol Venus. The traditional mythological images are hard to recognize. In addition, the characterizations of morning and evening star diverge so greatly that it is actually not possible to speak of *one* Venus symbol.

Here is still considerable need for research.

In the presentation of the planet symbol as a model here an attempt to display the two perspectives separately.

Some rulerships of the planet symbol Venus morning star as facet model
(ruler of the sign Taurus)

Some rulerships of the planet symbol Venus evening star as facet model
(ruler of the sign Libra)

This section is based in particular on the following literature, where further information can be found:

Gerlach, Wolfgang (Hrsg.), Publius Ovidius Naso. FASTI. Festkalender Roms, München 1960.

Mertz, Bernd A., Das große Handbuch der Astrologie, Sonderausgabe, München 1999.

Schäfer, Thomas, Bildersprache Astrologie, Wettiswil (CH) 1991.

Walter, Jörg, Entschlüsselte Aspektfiguren, Freiburg 1981.

Mars

Prehistory

The fourth planet of our solar system is also known as the red planet because it can be seen just above the horizon as a bright red celestial body, and thereof resulted its oldest name in Sumer: **Ṣimutu**, the deep red. In the 14th pre-Christian Century, the planet was attributed to Ninurta, the god of hunt and war, who was venerated in Nippur.

Ninurta hunting

Later it was assigned to Nergal, who before was astrologically connected to Saturn, a replacement, but for this change no reasons are known. The simultaneously appearing astrological interpretation of Mars as a planet of misfortune may be related to this changement – since there was never a connection with happy hunting. Nergal was considered the personified glowing summer heat, a war god and ruler of the underworld.

In Babylonian time Nergal was the city god of Kutha or Kuthu, a name, which also designates the Babylonian underworld.

Nergal with
lion's heads

According to the Bible people from Kutha have been forcibly resettled to Northern Palestine, and, mixed with Jews, who had not returned home after the Babylonian exile, they formed the people of the Samaritans.
(2 Kings 17, 24-30).

Pursuantly in Hebrew they are called Cuthim.

Nippur and Kutha
in the Babylonian
Empire

In Egypt hor–descher (red Horus) was the equivalent to Mars and regarded as being the living star of the sun god Re.

Because he also has times when he seems to be running backwards and the Egyptians could not foresee or calculate these, they called him an unreliable star.

Hor-dscher(u)/Hor-descher(u)

Mars-Hieroglyphs
(Hellenistic time)

In Greece, the red color became the namesake of the Pyrhoeis (the Red). But already Plato (424/423–348/347 BC) is said to have used the name "Star of Ares" in his epinomis. However, this association apparently was not made by Greeks, but by immigrated Chaldeans, who believed to have found a deity comparable to Nergal. They did not take in account that the Greek Ares had anything at all to do with the underworld.

In a similar way, based on superficial resemblances, further transfer was made to the Roman farmer god Mars.

MARS as a Roman god

Several derivations exist explaining the name of the god Mars. One of them is a reference made to Maris, the Etruscan god of love and fertility. Another one points out *Mawort, Latin MAVORS, an ancient Italian peasant god,who is regarded as the origin. After Radke (Gottesvorstellungen, pp 4) "... (the name) can be traced to a linguistic root, which describes the process of sharing;" (translation H. Goos) It means distribution of land among the peasants; this could explain the god's role in the VER SACRUM (see below p. 65). Cicero explains the name in his work DE NATURA DEORUM (About the nature of gods) as a contraction of MAGNA VERTO (I turn the great), because war inverts everything great.

The PIETAS ERGA DEOS (piety against the gods) transferred the attitude of full obedience committed to the biological father (even after his death) to the gods, who were invoked as PATER: Jupiter, Mars, Quirinus Janus, Neptunus, Liber, Falacer.

Performing their prescribed rites was a constant quasi childlike duty.

Mars belongs to the oldest Italian gods, its origin is Indo-European. In Rome he seems to have been worshipped from the early beginnings on. The name Marspiter was used in invocations as a contraction of Mars and Pater.

The three top state-employed priests (FLAMINES MAIORES) served the supreme male gods Jupiter, Mars and Quirinus. From this position of the three FLAMINES MAIORES former religious scientists have concluded there had been a so-called "Archaic triad" of Jupiter, Mars and Quirinus in early Roman history, followed by the later "Capitoline triad" of Jupiter, Juno and Minerva. But except for this conclusion no further evidence for such a construct could be found, so this hypothesis has been dropped.

Presumably, the appointment of these three chief priests served the peace between the initially competing members of the various tribes who had settled the hills of Rome; they respectively worshiped one of these deities as their supreme god (s. p. 7).

The high priest of Mars (FLAMEN MARTIALIS) was especially in charge for the consecration of the weapons of war. Intramural Mars was present in the form of a spear, which was stored in a special chamber, the SACRARIUM, of the REGIA (the head office of the High Priest). This seems to originate from the time when the Roman gods were not worshipped in pseudo-human form (similar to Jupiter the Stone, p. 70).

Some lances lay or stood in the same room and they stirred (vibrated) when the deity wished contact to his people – such a movement was immediately reported to the magistrate by the FLAMEN MARTIALIS. Before a campaign the respective commanders had to touch the weapons in this chamber and shout "MARS VIGILA!" (Mars wake up!) to summon the deity. There was also a sacred fire, which played an important role in the rite described below as "October horse".

The oldest shrine of Mars (ARA MARTIALIS) stood on the Field of Mars (CAMPUS MARTIUS), a more than 600 ac large area outside the first city wall, which was suitable for the deployment of the army. It served as a military training area and as the ceremonial welcome of foreign state guests who were not allowed to enter the city. Triumphal processions after successful conquests also were held here. From 100 BC on, however, the area was filled with buildings and incorporated into city borders under the Emperor Aurelian in the 3rd century AD.

As a defender of the city Mars was the god of the fit-to-fight citizens who were defending a settlement or city against human enemies. After the transition from citizen army into a professional army Mars receded into the background; this is also a result of the fact that in the in 509 AD consecrated Capitoline Temple Minerva was worshiped in his place (for political reasons, the conciliation of the Sabines in Rome certainly played a role).

So he was not involved in the first ritual meal for the gods (LECTISTERNIUM) 399 BC (participants: Apollo and Latona, Diana and Hercules, Mercury and Neptune); only at the great LECTISTERNIUM in 217 BC he is mentioned as a partner of Venus; this ritual was performed GRAECO RITU (according to Greek rite). This meant that the appropriate sacrifices were performed by bareheaded priests.

The fact that the gods were presented in the form of statues (likely made by Etruscan sculptors) and placed in pairs evidences strong Greek influence. Eating together sitting on the same sofa was following Roman ideas of decency impossible even for a married couple. Archeologic founds prove that this was an Etruscan habit. In 217 BC the previous combination of Mercury and Neptune was dissolved in favor of Mercury with Ceres and Neptune with Minerva.

The REGIA was a small building in the FORUM ROMANUM next to the Temple of Vesta. It is concluded from the name that it was the former royal residence, which the pontiff had taken over as subsequent REX SACRORUM after the end of the kingdom. It was destroyed several times by fire or earthquake, so that there are no archaeological evidences about its shape in the early days.

The Lectisternium of 217 BC was not organised by the COLLEGIUM PONTIFICUM, that was commonly responsible for the execution of ceremonies and sacrifices in RITUS PATRIUS (patriotic rite). It was organized by the same group, that consulted the Sibillini Books (s. p. 43): the DECEMVIRI SACRIS FACUNDIS. According to the origin of the oracle, the ritual was carried out in Greek Rite.

CONCORDIA group from 175 BC, placed nowadays in front of the
Roman Government building Palazzo Chigi

Under the influence of Greek oriented intellectuals Mars was often depicted
along with a goddess who was called Venus by later authors. However,
images of the two as a couple were called the "CONCORDIA Group", and
so it seems more likely that the goddess Concordia was meant.

In Sabine sources Mars is described "with his Nerio"; the transfer of
Greek religious patterns turned that into a goddess Nerio as his wife. However, it is comprehensible that "NERIO" is a Sabine expression of power
and strength and just describes a virtue of the god. This view is supported
by linguistical evidence.

After the decline of traditions in the late republican era followed by the
reign of Julius Caesar the cult of Mars returned to focus. As the 'father' of
Romulus and Remus, he plays an important role in the mythical founding
legend of the city of Rome, which became popular. Around the turn of
the eras, the magnificent temple of MARS ULTOR (Mars the avenger) was
consecrated in the Augustus Forum. This was accompanied by a certain
trivialization of the war god: Previously he was considered so terrible that
his shrine – and thus his sacrificial shite – had to reside outside the city
walls, but now, with the construction of this temple he was brought more
or less into the imperial center.

After Greek influence manifested itself in the Roman religion, Mars became like his "counterpart" Ares, mainly a god of war and companion of the army. As such, he was of course particularly revered by the soldiers, accordingly in almost all major garrison towns Mars temples were built

Clear status differences showed up: Ordinary soldiers worshipped Mars, officers were accustomed to (secret) Mithraism. Particularly for officers of plebeian origin, it was important for their career to become invited to join this cult.

The altar pictured to the right, found in Xanten and dated 55–68 AD, is dedicated to MARS CICOLLUS. Cicollus was a Gaulish god of power, the Romans equated him with Mars.

The inscription says:

"Dedicated to MARS CICOLLUS.
For the sake of the Emperor
(NERO CAESAR) AUGUSTUS,
conqueror of the Germanics and
father of the nation.
The Lingone citizens, who in CI(...)
have settled."

The Celtic people of the Lingones originate from Gaul (east France). They had a settlement near Xanten, which was destroyed 69 AD. Its name is indecipherable on the votive stone.

Mythological remains

Mars was already god of the Latins, when these were still peasants and shepherds. He was responsible for the protection of farms and fields against the untamed nature, the 'outside'. In this respect, he was responsible for health and fertility of the area protected by him, but not in the function of a fertility or healer god. His attributes were shield and spear.

As one of the oldest Roman gods Mars was often equated to Jupiter as MARSPITER (father Mars) in ceremonies.

During the reign of king Numa Pompilius (around 700 BC) Mars is said to have dropped his Holy Shield from heaven. In order that this could not be stolen 11 equal-looking shields were made, all 12 were kept in the SACRARIUM MARTIS (in the REGIA, see above). The priest council of Salians (SALII PALATINI) was responsible for them.

Historically it was probably the main god of the settlement on the Palatine Hill, although a shrine was never archaeologically proven there.

This was an association of 12 persons who had a meeting house on the Palatine Hill (a corresponding society for Quirinus resided on the Quirinal). The Palatine Salian dynasty formed the military attendants of MARS GRADIVUS (striding Mars). At celebrations in honour of him they wandered with the appropriate parades around the town and sang and danced at predetermined places according to a fixed protocol. They wore special ritual clothing, which probably corresponded to the soldier raiment of pre-Roman times. Their traditional song (CARMEN SALIARE) was so old that in historical times no one fully understood the text anymore. With shield and lance, they led a war dance according to an ancient, exactly

Mars-shield

prescribed ceremony. There are speculations that this singing and dancing was a banishing ritual against evil spirits, which thus made the Salians a kind of shaman assitants of the tutelary god. Even the interpretation that Mars as the incarnation of war should be kept out of the city by them is found in the literature.

Mars' holy animals were woodpecker, horse, bull and wolf, only male animals were allowed to be offered to him.

As the former patron god he was exclusively responsible for 'fair' wars (contrary to the Greek Ares); Caesar therefore made every effort to represent his campaigns north of the Alps as unaggressive.

In the provinces the INTERPRETATIO ROMANA equalized Mars, inter alios, with the Celtic Teutates and the Germanic Thincsus of the Tuihantes (Germanic people from a Dutch region).

This votive stone is an example of the mentioned Mars equation. It was found at Hadrian's Wall in England:

The inscription on the stone reads:

DEO
MARTI
THINCSO
ET DVABVS
ALAISAGIS
BEDE ET
FIMMILENE
ET N AVG GERM
CIVES TVIHANTI
V S L M

Translated:
To the god Mars Thincsus and the two Alaisiaga deities Beda and Fimmilena, and the divine spirit of the emperor, the Germanic tribesmen from the Tuihantes willingly and deservedly fullfilled their vow. (cited from GardenStone, Gods of the Germanic Peoples 2, p. 500)

Following Roman custom a foreign god like Thincsus was 'adopted' in the way, that one of the official Roman gods was equated to him, and so he became "Mars" Thincsus.

Cult

MARTIUS (March), the first month of the year after the old-Roman calendar, was named after and dedicated to Mars. Numerous celebrations in this month were performed for his veneration. Mars is honoured thereby as a Lord of the Beginnings: Beginning of the calendar year, beginning of arable farming, beginning of the time of military campaigns.

In 153 BC the commencement of the official year was postponed to January 1st.

On February 27th, the celebrations were opened with a horse race in honour of Mars, in the early days carried out as a riding event, later as a chariot race. Allegedly Romulus had donated this event in honour of his 'father' Mars.

MARSQUE CITOS IUNCTIS CURRIBUS URGET EQUOS;
EX VERO POSITUM PERMANSIT EQUIRRIA NOMEN,
QUAE DEUS IN CAMPO PROSPICIT IPSE SUO.
And Mars urges on his chariot's swift horses.
The day has retained the name Equirria,
From the horse races the god views on his fields.

Ovid: FASTI 2, 858-859, Translated by A. S. Kline

March 1st was the ancient Roman New Year's Day. The doors of public buildings, all the temples and statues of gods were decorated with fresh greenery. In the Temple of Vesta, the holy place of fire was cleaned, outside the buildings a new fire was kindled (with a wooden fire drill) and brought into the temple.

The people of Rome celebrated the event with a magnificent procession, in which the Salians performed their dances.

Housewives made gifts to their husbands and the female slaves were entertained by them with an opulent meal.

(MATRONALIA, counterpart to the SATURNALIA at December 17th.)

Many Mars rituals in March and October originate from a time, when martial activities took place only in the summer months.

March 9th was DIES RELIGIOSUS (religious day); the Salians carried the sacred shields of Mars around the entire city. The day was also a day of remembrance for MAMURIUS VETURIUS, the mythological blacksmith who forged the eleven copies of the shield.

Another performance took place this day, which is interpreted either as a winter expelling or scapegoat ritual: An elderly man in fur clothing was symbolically beaten with peeled willow twigs while driving him out of the city. This custom was so old that its real meaning is still unknown.

Campaigns began after the spring sowing and ended before beginning of the harvest. When Hannibal in the 2nd Punic War broke through this time pattern, largest confusion prevailed, because at the time of the invasion into the Po lowlands in December the Roman army had to be summoned quickly.

Salians in ancient combat clothing
carry the sacred shields to the dance place

Various rituals of Mars are so-called lustrations, ceremonial purifications and expiations. Following the social ideas of the psychoanalyst Donald Sandner, this may have been the effective Roman method to isolate and control the inevitable evil in society: If a community let "free run to the hate developing between humans and the hostilities resulting from it, it (the bad) would erode the entire social structure of the culture." (Translated from Donald Sandner, p. 161)

On March 17th, the celebrations for the start of the military season took place. At the REGIA (the seat of the highest priest) a ram was offered by the high priest and the tutelary gods of the state were invoked. Then a chariot race was held in honour of Mars either on the CAMPUS MARTIUS (Mars field) or later in the CIRCUS MAXIMUS.

On March 23th, these celebrations culminated in the TUBILUSTRIUM, the consecration of bugles or trumpets which were used as signal instruments for the army.

Roman bugle

On October 15th, the agricultural year ended with the sacrifice of the October Horse to Mars. The ritual began with a race of two-horse chariots on the CAMPUS MARTIUS. The entire population moved out of the city to see this spectacle.

The right horse of the winning chariot became the holy sacrifice to Mars, the god of war: The FLAMEN MARTIALIS killed it with a spear. Then, it was broken down very quickly and cut into three parts:

The **head** was surrounded with bread and either brought to the MAMILLIA Tower or to the REGIA. The use of bread suggests a form of thanksgiving for the protection guaranteed by Mars.

The **tail**, still bleeding, was brought into the REGIA, as fast as a runner could run, so that the blood could drip into the sacred fire burning there. For the use of the resulting ash there is some speculation, commonly it is assumed that it was later processed in the production of cleaning incense by the Vestals.

The **rest** of the Horse was prepared and consumed as usual with immolations.

On October 19th, the military season ended with the ceremonial cleansing of the weapons, the ARMILUSTRIUM. This was another 'religious day', a sacrifice to Mars was brought out at a shrine on the Aventine Hill and the Salians danced.

From the fact that the most important calendrically specified Mars rituals were military ones, the French scientist Dumézil concluded Mars had been a pure god of war without reference to agriculture. That view, however, disregards the alterations in Mars functions (see p. 59)

In addition to these as fixed calendar recorded occasions, there were more Mars rituals that were performed when needed.

SUOVETAURILIA were offerings of male animals in honour of Mars. In each case a Boar (SUS), a ram (OVIS) and a bull (TAURUS) were sacrificed. Apart from the events described below it was considered as general atonement and a cleansing ritual, e.g. after temple desecrations by enemies. Depending upon the importance of the event, dairy

SUOVETAURILIA

animals (SUOVETAURILIA LACTENTIA), yearlings (SUOVETAURILIA MINORA) or adult animals (SUOVETAURILIA MAIORA) were offered. A meat inspection after slaughter showed whether the sacrificed animal was faultless and the offer thereby valid, otherwise it had to be repeated.

Cato the Elder describes, how this ritual was performed as a spring ceremony by the farmers: A piglet, a lamb and a calf were led once around the entire property, afterwards dedicated and sacrificed to Mars in a solemn ceremony. The ritual was performed by the PATERFAMILIAS (head of the Family), it served as a cleansing of the fields after the winter and commitment of Mars as the protection god at the borders of the property.

Every five years, a similar ceremony for the whole population of Rome took place on the Mars Field (LUSTRUM = purification). All citizens of Rome (women and slaves not included) had to gather on the open space; they lined up in divisions according to the residential areas. They were then counted and the data recorded for the assessment of the tax. The sacrificial animals were here an adult boar, a ram and a bull. After these had paraded around all the people, they were ritually offered by the FLAMEN MARTIALIS.

At the time of the early Republic the same ceremony was performed in the CAMPUS MARTIUS before the departure of the home guard to a campaign with circumnavigation of the army by the sacrificial animals.

In imperial times a SUOVETAURILIA offer was a fixed part of the triumphal processions.

VER SACRUM (Holy Spring) was a sacrifice for the entire nation when in dire need in ancient Rome. It was told to have been performed for the last time in 217 BC, after the defeat of Cannae. All animals that were born in March and April of this year were dedicated to Mars and had to be sacrificed. This comprehensive offer is said to have led to the decisive victory in the 2nd Punic War.

Georges Dumézil has raised the hypothesis that the VER SACRUM was a general Indo-European custom, practised also by Celtic and Germanic peoples: If a tribe became too large for its area, they proclaimed a "Holy Spring". All young men of a certain age group, usually 20 or 21 years old, were dedicated to a god, as well as all animals that were born in a certain period of time.

In early Italy this god was Mamars, whose name became later shortened to Mars.

The dedicated group was then expelled from their people, chose a leader and moved away to establish a new tribe. The sanctified animals were thereby a kind of dowry. Mars was a guarantor for justice within the group during the settlement and distribution to the new homeland.

Cato the Elder

(CATO MAJOR, 234–149 BC), born as Marcus Porcius Cato was a Roman senator and historian known for his conservatism and opposition to Hellenization. He was the first to write history in Latin.

Georges Dumézil

(1898 – 1986)

was a French theologian and sociologist who explored the archaic Roman religion and brought it into connection with other Indo-European traditions.

From the ages given, we can conclude that the men were married, so entire families moved away.

The migrating group chose a Mars-sacred animal as a 'leader'. They followed it and marked their new living space where it settled down in the wilderness.

Often, they named the new tribe after this totem animal.

The Roman version of the VER SACRUM in 217 BC, reported by Livy consisted – as usual – a vow to Mars and the sacrifice of all animals born in March and April of this year on the Mars Field. Livy expressly emphasized that human sacrifice had been renunciated. (Livy XXXIII)

Wolf, leading animal of the Romans

Names of tribes that are said to origin from a VER SACRUM:

- The **Hirpins** after HIRPUS, the wolf in Sabine language.
- The **Picines** after PICUS, the woodpecker.
- The **Vultures** after VULTUR, the geier.
- The **Aeques** or **Aequicoles** after EQUUS, the horse.
- The **Samnites** are told to be guided by a bull, that is why their capital is called BOVIANUM after the Latin BOS (bovine); it was founded on the hill where the animal had led them.
- The **Mamertini** on Sicily traced their name directly to that of the god Mars.

Dumézil claims – referring to this hypothesis and Livy's description – to have also detected evidence that the foundation of Rome was based on a VER SACRUM with Romulus as leader of the group and the she-wolf as totem animal.

Considering the previous, the importance of Mars for the Romans is clear. He was not just MARS GRADIVUS, the god who progressed in war, he was also guarantor of the frontiers gained. Augustus made him MARS ULTHOR the avenger of Caesar's murder.

However, his main function seems to have been the periodic purification of both soldiers and war material: All abominations that war brings were thus removed and especially the involved humans remained untainted. Although the social importance for the community declined accordingly to the deduction of the civil army, the existing rituals remained. With their help, the Romans were sure to have only fought in just wars and to rule almost the entire known western world legitimately.

Mars in Astrology

The Swedish scientist Carl Linnaeus (1707–1778) introduced the astronomical symbol for Mars as label "male" and the sign for Venus as "female" into biology.

Nowadays looking for the keyword "Mars" in relevant encyclopaedias, the fourth planet of our solar system is specified first. The 'red planet' has this name since Roman times. The abbreviation used for it is a circle with an arrow right above ♂, the same character that is used in biology for male.

As an explanation for this glyph, it can be imagened well that a pulse (arrow) outgoing from matter (circle) is depicted. This is also the basic content of the planetary symbol of Mars in astrology, as it is understood today. Mars symbolizes the operating energy that exists in every human.

> For each activity energy is needed, without which nothing can be undertaken.

The astrological Mars rules the sign Aries. From spring Equinox in March the Sun stays there for about 30 days. Aries is the first sign of spring, the symbol for awakening and new beginnings.

It is not the vitality that is associated with the Sun concerned here, but the energy to stand up, to progress. Courage and ambition are signs of this energy, but also blind dash off, and aggression. The concretisations of the Marsian pulse can be learned from more than 2000 tags to Mars in the "Lexikon der astrologischen Zuordnungen" (rulership book).

The position of Mars in the individual horoscope not only shows the strength of existing Mars power, but also how it can be realized. Since Mars energy results from matter, it is expressed usually in a physical way. The 'invention' of sport in the 19th century can be well thought of as a response to the increase of power-saving machines in the world of work. Sports today compensate the decreased need of physical power at work for many people. Athletes typically have a disproportionately high level of operating power.

Blocked Mars energy can show a tendency to sudden outbursts of aggression against the environment and people ("intermittent explosive disorder"), but also self-destruction in the form of self-harm ("skin-cutting") or unreflected foolhardiness is possible. Although not blocked, but used unproductively Mars potential shows a lack of perseverance, which causes current projects not to be finished and, instead, new projects started and left unfinished too.

Courageous behaviour is indeed quite a characteristic of active Mars energy, in the positive case not without assessment of risk, which is then reduced accordingly through appropriate arrangements.

How much the use of positive Mars energy can carry out, can be demonstrated in the horoscope of Mahatma Gandhi. In his natal chart there shows an especially high potential. Without this internal strength life and success of the peace fighter would not have been possible.

In Central Europe for the first time in history for more than seventy years no war has taken place (and foreseeably will not take place), therefore the formerly manifested Mars energy must realize itself in other forms. Already twenty years ago the astrologer Manfred Michael Herm has in his lectures on mundane Astrology pointed out that the collective and individual energy potential, the Martian energy, does not simply disappear in peaceful times. As already mentioned, sport, especially mass sport is certainly one of the positive social valves. But also negative developments such as aggressive hooligans, rampages and fisticuffs on diverse occasions have to account for unsolved Mars energy. Social solutions need to be found to counteract this and use it profitably instead.

The planet Mars is also a symbol for the journey into the unknown, the desire to discover new things and the inaptitude to live always and only in the same routine. This makes people with high Mars energy pulse generators in society, without them there would be no further development.

Summary

The archetypal Mars in modern western astrology has little in common with the Roman god of war Mars. But in MARS GRADIVUS, the one who progresses the troupe, a similarity can be seen shining through. The central idea in the Roman function of the active protector to the outside is so far not covered by the astrological symbol of Mars, but is also not contained in any other planet symbol.

Perhaps this is a reflection of actual social conditions: as the incidents concerning espionage and cybercrime in recent years have shown, we are obviously vulnerable to the subjection of spying even in private life. While the main focus rarely lies on physical threat, influence on our behaviour and control of our needs up to so-called 'brainwashing' are certainly the intention of the initiators. Defence here would be the new field of activity for unneeded (war) energy. But a Mars potential used for military attacks for centuries can probably not reverse the polarity within a few decades, especially since many nations outside Europe have not yet begun such a change.

The Roman religion provides advice, as to which direction the use of the existing force could go. The Romans have successfully defended their 'social' Mars against the brainless onrushing Ares, who partly acted in a spirit of mischief. The task of our society is individually and collectively, to show how martial mental power can be lived as physical sporting exercise, as environmental activity, as a renewal movement, etc., without bringing negative aggressive sides to the activity. Astrology can support this process with individual advice and mundane analysis.

In alchemy ♂ denotes not only the red planet, but also its associated metal iron, the basic material of war weapons.

How warlike Mars energy inadvertently still exists, is demonstrated for example, by the German federal army, decidedly founded as a defensive troop, but yet again prepared for attack as part of its armament.

Mars with shield and spear

Some rulerships of the planet symbol Mars as facet model

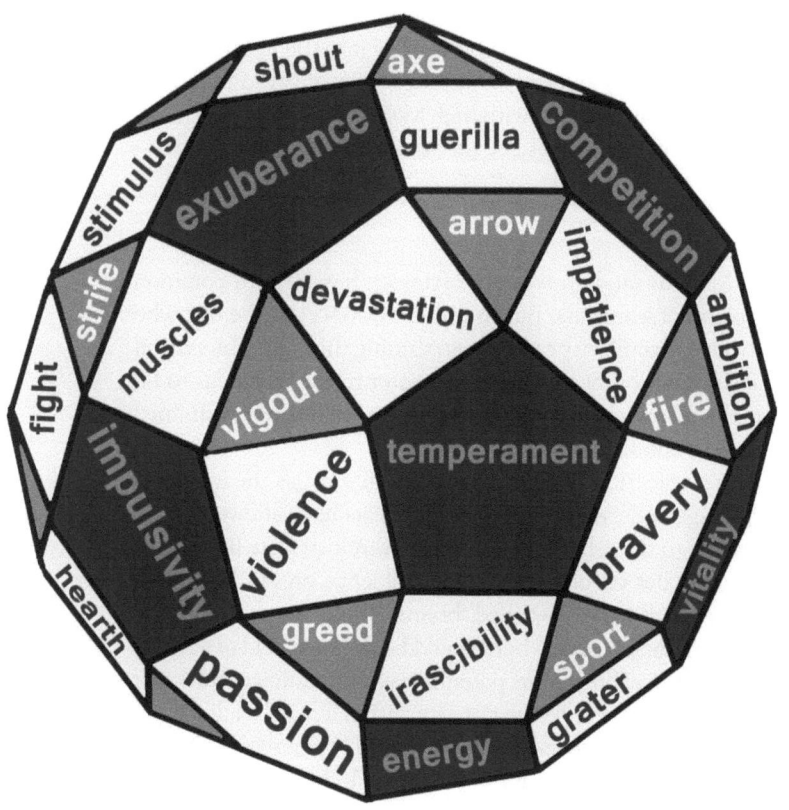

This section is based in particular on the following literature, where further information can be found:

Dumezil, Georges, Archaic Roman Religion, translated from French by Philip Krapp, Baltimore 1996.

A. S. Kline's FREE Poetry Archive, Publius Ovidius Naso, FASTI

Müller, Volker, Römische Religionsgeschichte, Universität München, Fachdidaktik klassische Philosophie, WS 2010-11.pdf

Radke, Gerhard, Zur Entwicklung der Gottesvorstellung und der Gottes-verehrung in Rom, Darmstadt 1987.

Jupiter

Prehistory

The fifth and largest planet in our solar system was called **sag.me.gar** (meaning unknown) among the Sumerians and **mul.bab.bar**(white star) by the Babylonians. It was the star of the god Marduk, the city god of Babylon and chief god of the Babylonian pantheon. Marduk is the one who has created the earth. Thereto he has killed his grandmother Tiamat and formed the world out of her body. Humans are his creatures according to some versions of the Mesopotamian creation myth.

He is master of the forces of nature, dictates the four winds, the fire and the lightning, but his strongest weapon is the flood.

In the descriptions he often acts like a violent tyrant over gods and men.

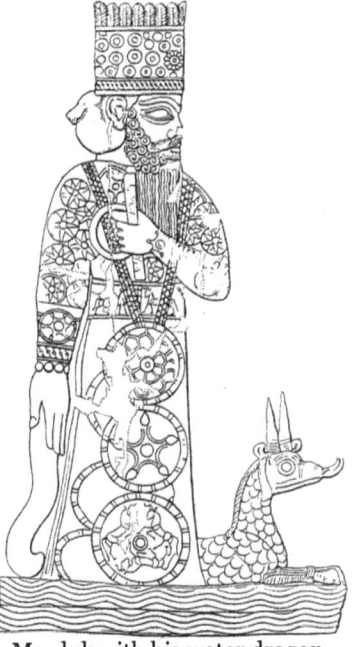

Marduk with his water dragon

Following the Mesopotamian creation myths Marduk became entrusted with the panels of fate which determine the history of the world.

Hor-wepesch-taui

Jupiter hieroglyphe
Old Kingdom

In Egypt, around 1450 BC, the planet is mentioned in inscriptions as hor-wepesch-taui "he who illuminates the sky". The deity Osiris may have been assigned to him. There is also evidence of a link to Re. As a relatively bright star, this planet was known to the Egyptians for a long time.

Among the early Greeks, the 5th planet initially had the common name Phaethon (the shining). This planet name may be a translation from Egyptian and has nothing to do with the mythological figure of Phaeton, son of the sun god Helios.

After the astrological school of Berosos, with corresponding Babylonian impact, gained increased influence, the planet became the star of Zeus who was seen analogous to Marduk.

As a result of the INTERPRETATIO ROMANA, the Roman god IUPPITER was equated to him.

According to Greek mythology Phaeton was a young man, who tried to control the solar car of his father Helios and thus provoked a catastrophe. In modern comparisons his name refers to a symbol for hubris.

IUPPITER as a Roman god

From linguistic research
the hypothesis originates
that there was a generally
common Indo-European
sky god.
This *dieu may
be derived from
conforming Greek *Zeus*
with the Indian *Dyaus*,
the Latin *Iuppiter* and the
German *Tyr* or *Ziu*.

A supreme heavenly god *Diu, Diovis* seems to have been common to all the Italic peoples, because he cannot be found exclusively among Oskens, Sabellens, Umbrians or Latins. However, the connection with -PATER (-father) to IUPPITER is only made by Romans and Umbrians.

IUPPITER (sometimes IUPITER) is the supreme god of the Romans. In art, in particular the statues created by Etruscan craftsmen, and in literary tales he is equated to the Greek Zeus. However, he retained uniqueness in his cult.

Not only Latin students stumble upon the fact that the supreme god of the Romans has apparently two names (see table on the right).

In title and in invocations he is the heavenly father, IUP-PITER; linguistically integrated into formulations IOVIS is used. This has evolved from the old Latin DIOVIS "belonging to the day". The phrase SUB IOVE "under the open sky" matches this.

Latin grammatical use of the name Jupiter		
case	English	Latin
nominative	(the) Jupiter	IUPPITER
vocative	Oh Jupiter!	IUPITER!
accusative	(ask) Jupiter	IOVEM
genitive	Jupiter's	IOVIS
dative	(for) Jupiter	IOVI
ablative	(by) Jupiter	IOVE

The supplements in brackets were added for a better understanding.

Expressed in the name is that Jupiter is a god of light and the celestial vault. This is expressed by the epithet IUPPITER LUCETIUS ("the shining one") that was used mainly for religious ceremonies.

Jupiter was probably already worshiped by the Italians of the Neolithic Age. This is indicated through the use of flint knives to seal a contract in his name; an archaic custom, which throughout the Copper Age, the Bronze Age, and the introduction of iron tools had survived.

Flint is a hard silicate
that was used to knock
off sparks for making fire
from pyrite.

This fits perfectly with a
deity whose feature is the
lightning flash.

Flint (Silex)

During this ceremony the god seems to have been identified with the stone, because the contractual partners swore whilst it by IOVEM LAPIDEM "Jupiter the Stone". The sequence of such a ritual is described on page 82.

The identification of Jupiter with flint can be seen as analogous to Mars as a spear (s. p. 57).

As the highest god of an agrarian people he of course oversaw the most important natural phenomenon for farmers: the weather. He sent lightning (IUPPITER FULGUR), thunder (IUPPITER TONANS), sunshine (IUPPITER SERENUS) winds and rain (IUPPITER PLUVIALIS). Therefore, he was included in all religious ceremonies of the rural population.

When a thunderstorm with lightning and thunder went down he grudged. Only after the Etruscan doctrine of prediction by lightning observation was introduced in Rome, this natural phenomenon was taken in account differently. The bundle of flashes remained however Jupiter's attribute, places where lightning had gone down, were regarded as holy property of the god and were ordained in a special ceremony.

Also his second traditional competence results from peasant life: the boundary stones. Nothing is more important for a farmer than the size of his fields and this was marked by boundary stones. Jupiter was patron of the city of Rome from the beginning on, his presence in the city was symbolized by corresponding stones.

In Rome, there were three Jupiter-sacred stones:

- The LAPIS TERMINALIS in the Capitoline Jupiter Temple, according to a legend it stood there already before the temple was built. Because it couldn't be moved, the temple was built around it and above its place an opening in the roof, so that the stone continued standing 'open-air'. It is regarded as the guardian of the city borders; some authors claim that it symbolizes a predecessor god of Jupiter.
- The LAPIS MANIALIS ("the stone to flow") was needed at the AQUAELICIUM, a rain summoning ceremony to end drought periods. Then the stone, usually positioned at the via Appia, was carried through the town. But later, in the imperial era, this ritual had been fallen into oblivion.
- The TERMINUS SANCTUS (Holy Stone), the 6th milestone on the VIA LAURENTINA, regarded as symbolic city boundary. Religious scholars are at odds of whether

Personificated TERMINUS

TERMINUS was a discreet, originally Sabine god or the personification of a Jupiter function. There is evidence for both.

All these stones stood in the open air.

In contrast to his Greek counterpart Zeus, Jupiter obviously didn't need to prove his manhood physically. He is a bachelor.

Of course, the supreme god in a world which is dominated by men can be only male – but neither in mythological stories, nor in the rite is his gender emphasized by the Romans. This is all the more remarkable as the worship of the Italic god of Heaven can be traced back till the Neolithic thus into the time of the cult of Magna Mater.

As the highest divine guardian of the city and its inhabitants the god was addressed as IUPPITER OPTIMUS MAXIMUS.

The oldest Roman Jupiter temple is said to have been established by Romulus on the Capitol and dedicated to IUPPITER FERETRIUS. The meaning of this epithet remains unknown, only speculations exist.

Alleged ruins of the Temple of IUPPITER FERETRIUS

Mythological remains

The god manifested his will in the flight of birds and in the form of lightning, both phenomena in the sky. For the interpretation of the divine omen there was a special college of priests, the augurs. Their function wand was the crook, the LITUUS.

As far as can be deduced from the preserved rites, Jupiter was first the god of everything that belongs to the sky: light and rain at the right time, bird flight and lightning, but also thunderstorms, tempest and probably hail. The offerings of various peasant feasts served to persuade him to refrain from harmful actions. The inclusion of Jupiter in all rituals in favour of crops and good harvest has in the past led to consider him as a vegetation god. However, this could not really be proven, the offers to Jupiter during all rural rituals are today explained that he had to be considered always as the supreme god of the pantheon.

In contrast to this all the archaeological testimonies of Jupiter worship do not originate from rural surroundings, but from cities. There stood the Jupiter temples in which he was believed to be present. In contrast to Tinia, the highest god of the Etruscans, Jupiter has no relation to the underworld.

Pliny mentions (with reference to Varro) the appeasement of storms as main purpose of the Vinalia in August (after Dumézil, p. 184)

Although Jupiter's name identifies him as the Indo-European sky god, his old-Italic manifestations are more likely faced towards the earth. He resides not high up on an Olympus, quasi between heaven and earth, but in temples amidst the human settlements. These edifices were erected generally on the highest point of the community, but this is an arrangement which can be found often in many cultures for holy places and also for Christian churches.

But the god could manifest himself in humans too, they then embodied Jupiter's greatness and power for a period of time. In the legend this is said

Monte Cavo, central summit of the Alban Hills.
On its top in ancient times the temple of JUPITER LATIARIS was erected,
on the slopes of the mountain the city of ALBA LONGA stretched out.

Livy reports that Romulus
spoke TAMQUAM
CAELESTI VOCE "like a
celestial voice" and thus
called the army to
resistance and final
victory
(AB URBE CONDITA I,12)

to have happened with Romulus, when he invoked IUPPITER STATOR in a battle during the wars between Latins and Sabines. The victory parades of later triumphators were an embodiment of the deity as well, the celebrated ones wore the clothes taken off from the god statue, kept its imperial insignia in their hands and were driven standing on a Quadriga (chariot drawn by four horses abreast) all along the VIA SACRA to the Temple of Jupiter on Capitoline Hill – virtually 'home'.

The highest Jupiter priest, the FLAMEN DIALIS was subject to many restrictions, making it clear that he officially acted as the god Jupiter. Therefore he must not be 'maculated' with anything earthly. This ritual purity, which was a consideration for other priests during a sacrifice, was the permanent state of the FLAMEN DIALIS. There were countless rules for his every day life, all of which in order to maintain his 'holiness', which should be consolidated by a state of perpetual holiday. Even the sight of working people was forbidden to him; a bellman had to precede him in town, so that work could stop when he passed.

The rules included his family, too. Both his and his wife's parents had to live in a CONFARREATIO marriage and the priest was married also after this rite. His wife, the FLAMINICA, had also religious obligations, sacrificial acts as well as accompanying of her husband in public performances.

Although the appointment of the FLAMEN DIALIS was lifelong, he had to resign when his wife died (this can be explained by the fact that without the FLAMINICA DIALIS the ARGEI rites could no longer be properly performed, see p. 94).

A marriage in Rome could be contracted in three forms:

COEMPTIO ('buy')
Symbolic sale of the daughter by the father in front of witnesses.

COHABITATIO or USUS
Confirmation of an existing relation by a public speech of the groom.

CONFARREATIO
Marriage as a holy act with sacrifice of a spelt cake, in the presence of the PONTIFEX MAXIMUS and other witnesses.

Without existing Roman Jupiter myths we have to extrapolate his special meanings from documented epithets. There are four groups:

Epithets of Honour (COGNOMINA HONORIS):

OPTIMUS MAXIMUS abbreviated as O. M. is an additive for the epithets of honour used almost always behind the Name.

Epithet	Translation	Meaning
OPTIMUS MAXIMUS	highest greatest	general honorific salutation
AEDES	era	ruling the era
CAELESTIS	heavenly	god of the sky
CULMINALIS	culminating	standing at the top
DAPALIS	dining	oblation receiver
DEFENSOR	defender	highest, most powerful defender
DEPULSOR	back thrower	enemies back thrower
EPULUS	regaled one	regaled as honoured guest
ELICIUS	down dragged one	He who descended from heaven, worshipped in Aventine Hill temple
EXSUPERANTISSIMUS	most outstanding	outstanding everything
FRUGIFER	fruitful	
IMPULSOR	push giving	drive giving
INVICTUS	invincible	
LUCETIUS	light supporting	light carrier
MAIUS	highest	
MEILICHIOS	sweet as honey	
MONITOR	warner	supreme mightiest warner
OPITULATOR	helper	helper in need
PANTHEUS	universal	combines all the gods in himself
PATER PATRATO	father, paternal	father of all fathers
PRAESTES	surpassing	above everything
PROPAGATOR	spreader	highest expander, enhancer
PURPURIO	purple decorated	supreme highest purple wearer (a ruler's cloak was decorated purple)
SALUTARIS	salvific	highest salvific
SEMPITERNUS	eternal	
SERVATOR	sustainer	
SOTER	saviour	
SUMMUS	top	supreme god of the pantheon
VALENS	value possessing	supreme valuable

Epithets of action (NOMINA ACTIONIS):

Epithet	Translation	Meaning
ADVENTUS	coming	the coming (expected)
ALMUS	consoling	the comforter
AMARANUS	bitter	carrying (away) bitterness
COHORTALIS		protector of the cohort
CONSERVATOR	protector	protector and sustainer
CULTOR	served one	he who receives the service
CUSTOS	doorkeeper	guardian of (entry) door
FARREUS	marriage con-firmer	guarantor of the CONFARREATIO marriage (see above p. 73)
FERETRIUS	spoils carrying (?)	Recipient of the armour taken from the (defeated) enemy's leader
FIDIUS	faithful	guarantor of observance of agreements and treaties
FULGUR, FULGURATOR. FULMINATOR	lightning, lightning thro-wer	shows his will in flash, catapults daytime lightning
INDIGES	procreative	forefather
INVENTOR	inventor	originator
IURARIUS	sealer	protector of oaths
IUTOR	judge	highest judge
IUVENTAS	youth	protector of the youth
LAPIS	stone	firm as the holy Jupiter stone
LIBERATOR	liberator	originally liberator from winter
PATRONO	patron	protector
PISTOR	miller or baker	recipient of bread offerings (?)
PECUNIA	money	protector or bringer of money
PLUVIUS, PLUVIALIS	rain, raining	rain maker
PREDATORE	capturer	spoil gainer (for the winner in war)
PROPUGNATOR	defender	Jupiter the warrior
PURGATOR	justifying	the legitimating
RECTOR	leader	he who shows the direction
REDUX	retired	patron of veterans
RESTITUTOR	restorer	restorer of justice
RIGATOR. REGATUR	watering	the mead watering
SENIO	6 giver at dice	donator of game luck

The listed **epithets of action** provide a comprehensive picture of the responsibilities of the Roman god Jupiter.

In particular, the conversion from a weather god to the highest city god of a complex society becomes clear.

Epithet	Translation	Meaning
SERENUS, SERENATOR	pleasant weather	bringer of good weather (revered in Pesaro)
SOSPES	safe and sound	caring for welfare
STATOR	making standingr	giving strength and stability in the face of adversity
TEMPESTANS	storming	storm god
TERRITOR	terrifyer	
TONANS, TONITRATOR	thundering, thunderer	master of lightning and thunder
VERSOR	turner	turning fate (for the better)
VICTOR	winner	helper to victory
VINDEX	bailsman	guarantor for the just cause

Epithets from the place of worship:

Here arises the conjecture, that the name IUPPITER not always pointed to the same, distinct god, but instead can be regarded as a general title for the highest god in the Latinspeaking world as shown in the table of equatings on the next page.

Epithet	Translation	Place or worshippers
ANXUR		Volscian Anxur (Terracina)
APENINUS	Apennine	Sabines in the mountains
ARCANUS	holy	holy shrines of Praeneste
ATTINUS		Sabines
BELENO		Peligni (Abruzzo)
CAELIUS		temple on Caelian Hill (Rome)
CAPITOLINUS		temple on Capitoline Hill (Rome)
CIMINUS		temple in Cimino
DOMESTICUS	domestic	household family altar
ELIOPOLITANO		temples in Heliopolis
FAGUTALIS	belonging to beeches	temple on Esquiline Hill (Rome) (in a beech grove)
FAZIUS	fateful (?)	temples in Campania
FISIU		temples in Umbria
FLADIUS,		temple in Cuma
FLAGIUS	flag (?)	temple in Capua
IGUVIUM		tutelary god of the city Iguvium in Umbria
LARENE		Peligni (Abruzzo)
LATIARIS, LATIUS	latin	tutelary god of the Latins (temple on Mons Albanus, see p. 73)
MOURCUS		Puglia
PAGANICUS	rural	farmer villages

Epithet	Translation	Place or worshippers
PALENI		Peligni (Sulmo)
RUMINUS	Roman	Etruscan name of Rome's City god (in Etruscan *u* stands for *o*)
TIFATINUS		Campania
VESUVIUS		Campania
VIMINUS		Temple on Viminal Hill (Rome)

Jupiter-Epithets of equating with other gods
(INTERPRETATIO ROMANA):

Epithet	respective deity
AMMONIO	in Libya venerated form of Bacchus
ANTIPADRO	dethroner of PATER SATURNUS
CACUNUS	mythical figure from pre-Roman times
CLITUMNUS	Umbrian god Cltunno
DIANUS	double-faced Janus
DOLICHENUS	semitic Hadad-Baal-Teshub
LIBER	peasant god of growth and sprouting, later equated as IUPPITER LIBERATOR
SABATIO	tutelary god of (Anguillara) Sabazia
SERAPIS	tutelary god of the Ptolemaic Empire
SCOTIA	worship form of hekate in Egypt
SOTER	suspected connection with a Sun god
SUCCELLUS	Celtic god Sucellus
SUMMANUS	former opponent of the day-god Jupiter as nightly lightning thrower
TERMINUS	god of boundaries; by inclusion of the stone embodying him in the temple of Jupiter on Capitol Hill he is equated with him.
VEIOVIS, VEDIOVIS	Ve-Iovis, may be an underground god, the meaning of the prefix is unknown.

In addition to the forms of invocation, which highlight Jupiter as the highest of the Roman pantheon, the action names show that this god is a guarantor of order and justice, protector of those in need, ideal leader and bringer of luck.

The archaic function of the weather god was left behind, a natural development in the context the of urbanization of the Romans. Nevertheless, the traditional form of "flash's funeral" stayed, i. e. marking a place hit by a flash with a grave-like stone (PUTEAL), marking it this way as in possession and taken by Jupiter himself.

In contrast to his astrological 'predecessors' Marduk and Zeus, the Supreme god of the Romans did not win his position through a combat with an ancestor. He is not at all a fighting god, but gains his power from his role as guardian of the legal order. In this role, he is guarantor of legitimacy in the Roman State, and at the same time its maintainer.

Marduk

fought against his grandmother Tiamat and is recognized by the other "younger" gods as leader of the Pantheon after his victory.

Zeus

fought together with the cyclopes and hundred-armed giants liberated by him against the titans under the leadership of his father Cronus. After he had defeated them, he became supreme Olympic god.

Marduk fights

Being such an important vital link for the social cohesion, it perhaps even was the dismissal of Jupiter in favour of SOL INVICTUS as "Lord of the Roman Empire" (DOMINUS IMPERII ROMANI) in the year 274 AD that led to the decline of the Roman state and culture forming the breeding ground for the emergence of Christianity.

The FLAMEN DIALIS was the only Roman priest with political rights.

» He had a seat in the senate,

» he was entitled to sit on a special sort of throne, the SELLA CURULIS,

» he was accompanied by a personal LICTOR and

» he wore lifelong the TOGA PRAETEXTA bordered with purple stripes.

Cult

As already mentioned, Jupiter as the highest god was seen as present in some form in all religious ceremonies. But of course there were also celebrations, which were performed only for him.

The central person in Jupiter rituals was the FLAMEN DIALIS; after the REX SACRORUM he was the second highest priest on Capitol Hill. The age of this religious custodianship can be deduced from the many partly archaic and even contradictory rules. Opposite to all other Roman state priests, he doesn't bear the name of the god represented by him. Literally translated his denomination means 'high priest of the day', as if Jupiter was himself the embodiment of the (bright) day in contrast to the night.

FLAMEN
with his typical head covering, the APEX

The **IDUS IOVI** determined the calendar in early times. Back then, all full moon days were holy to Jupiter, i.e., those days when the nights do not become dark. IDUS (or EIDUS) meant first division, i. e. the division of the month in two halves, later became it the word for full moon. Ides thus originally concerned the three days, on which the moon appears full. They were placed as holidays into the centre of the calendrical month.

This makes it obvious again that Jupiter is seen as a sky god, more exactly, a god of the brightness. According to the Roman philosopher Macrobius (s. p. 96) the actual full moon day was called also IOVIS FIDUCIA (confidence in Jupiter). The most important Jupiter ritual on this day was sacrificing a white male lamb by the FLAMEN DIALIS in presence of the REX SACRORUM and other high priests. The sacrificial animal was led first following the VIA SACRA through the whole city to the Capitol and offered there in front of the ARX, the old castle. This sacrificial site shows that the ritual already must have taken place before building the Jupiter temple in 506 BC.

The day was a public holiday, with no work even for slaves. The following day was considered especially unfavourable for business dealings (DIES ATER).

In this Roman calendar document the entry EIDUS can be recognized in the middle of each month. It is probably the oldest existent one.

Full Moon is always when the earth is exactly in the middle between sun and moon. The moon orbits the earth in 27.3 days. Since during this time the earth on its orbit also moves further, full moon is every 29.53 days.

FASTI ANTIATES MAIORES
Painted wall-calendar from the late Roman republic
created between 67 and 55 BC

When on occasion of a calendar reform in the 5th century BC the orientation on the lunar cycle had been abandoned, the expression IDUS for the 13th or 15th day of each month remained. Although it concerned only *one* public holiday, IDUS remained a word that only exists in plural (grammatically a plural word). So in the middle of each month there was a Jupiter-feast. During the months of March, May, July and October it was the 15th, in the other ones the 13th day.

It should be kept in mind that the 7-day week with the free Sunday was only introduced by the Emperor Constantine in 321 AD.

The most common calendars in ancient times consisted of continuous working days with feast days distributed irregularly over the year.

79

In addition, there were more scheduled and unscheduled festivities in honour of the supreme Roman god.

From 13th to 15th February, the LUPERCALIA were celebrated, a presumably maturity ritual, which originated in pre-Roman times so far in the past that its meaning was no longer understood by the Romans. It was the task of the FLAMEN DIALIS to slaughter two goats and a dog as sacrifices. This is all the more remarkable because goats and all their products otherwise were taboo for the priest of Jupiter. Boys called LUPERCI ran on defined courses through the city and with fur strips they hit females passing by who intentional presented themselves for that.

A sacrifice of something to drink (LIBATIO) was usually made by pouring the wine with the SIMPULUM, a round bowl with long shaft, from the mixing bowl (CRATER) into the sacrificial Bowl (SIMPUVIUM).

As a simple ritual the first sip from ones own drinking cup was poured on the earth.

On April 23th, the VINALIA PRIORA were celebrated. Not before this day the wine from the grapes of the previous year was allowed to be brought into the city for consumption. The first cup was sacrificed as unmixed wine in a special bowl, the CALPAR by the FLAMEN DIALIS. This sacred wine was ordained to Jupiter, profane wine (mostly mixed and seasoned) was under the seal of Venus (see p. 48).

On May 5th, the Latin Festival (FERIAE LATINAE) took place on MONTE CAVO in the temple of IUPPITER LATIARIS. A bull was sacrificed to Jupiter. By size and wealth of their embassy the participating Latin towns expressed their power and strength. Rome gained early a special position since Roman priests could decide whether the sacrifice was valid or not (Livy 41, 16, 2).

On July 5th, the POPLIFUGIA are registered as Jupiter festival in the calendar. About its meaning much is speculatd, except for the sacrifice brought on this day nothing further is recorded.

On August 19th, the VINALIA RUSTICA were celebrated. The FLAMEN DIALIS opened the vintage with the sacrifice of a female white sheep and at the same time cutting the first grape, crushing the fruits by hand and offer the juice likewise. This wine festival was hold also for Venus (see p. 48).

Since the same date is also DIES NATALIS (birthday) of the temple of VENUS OBSEQUENS, contemporary Roman writers report differently as to which deity was in charge here. The gender of the sacrificial animal allows the conclusion of a goddess. Otherwise the engagement of the FLAMEN DIALIS makes this event definitely a Jupiter-ritual. A religious ceremony in favour of the weather god is easily explained through the accompanying circumstances. Only good weather – not too dry, not too wet, no storms, no hail – makes a successful grape harvest possible.

Architectural relief plague – vintage and tramping grapes.
Rome 2nd half 1 c. AD

In addition, there is no reason why on this day only one deity should have been considered. The shared sacrifice trench between Venus and Jupiter temple on the Capitol shows clearly that there was a connection between these two deities, though about its nature nothing more is known.

On October 7th, there was the feast of IUPPITER FULGUR ET TONANS, during which everybody tried to imitate thunder with many instruments. This is said to have been fun and a reason for real noise competitions. Perhaps it was originally based on a summoning ritual against heavy thunderstorms occurring in autumn.

On October 11th, the Romans celebrated the MEDITRINALIA, the third wine festival. It is believed that with the in this times usual wine fermentation methods, the first young wine was now complete. This is an indispensable presupposition to explain that the focus of this festival was the mixture of 'old and new' wine.

An **aetiological invention** is used in order to explain the reason for a current status because the real causes are no longer known.

With more than 400 gods and goddesses in the Roman Empire the assumption, that such a goddess existed, was quite plausible.

The name of the ceremony probably derives from Latin MEDENDO (for what is to heal). in later times (2nd century AD) SEXTUS POMPEIUS FESTUS propagated a health goddess MEDITRINA.

Modern religious scholars assume, however, that she is an aetiological invention.

At this festival a libation was donated first and that blessed the new wine. Then, the above described mixture was imbibed under recitation of the following 'spell':

NOVUM VETUS VINUM BIBO
NOVO VETERI MORBO MEDEOR
(I'm drinking new and old wine
in order to be healed from new and old sickness)

VARRO, DE LINGUA LATINA 6,21

Thus the mixture was said to have a special healing power.

In addition to these calendrically scheduled Jupiter rituals there were a lot more, depending the occasion. The most important ones were related to his role as guarantor of treaties and agreements:

- Although not scheduled, but in any case shortly after taking office, the new consuls had to make a sacrifice to IUPPITER LATIARIS on MONS ALBANUS following an ancient rite.

- When a boy became adult and thus took off the juvenile TOGA PRAETEXTA, he sacrificed to Jupiter.

The status of a male Roman patrician could be read from his toga: Minors wore the (with purple stripes decorated) TOGA PRAETEXTA, adults a pure white Toga.

- Every religious act began with an invocation of Jupiter. An example can be found in Cato's DE AGRICULTA (agr. 134,2):

This emerges the question, if the purple edged Togas of the high priests meant that they belong to a god the same way as a minor to his father.

> IUPPITER, TE HOC FERTO OBMOVENDO
> BONAS PRECES PRECOR, UTI SIES VOLENS
> PROPITIUS MIHI LIBERISQUE MEIS DOMO
> FAMILIAEQUE MACTUS HOC FERTO.
>
> Translated:
> Jupiter, to you I offer this gift
> I ask you amicably: Be benevolent and
> gracious to me and my children, to the house
> and the clan, affirmed by this gift.

A religious act for more than one deity ended with an invocation of Vesta.

- Government and civil contracts were concluded in front of the temple of IUPPITER FERETRIUS, storage place of silex (see p. 70). Thereby it was sworn PER IOVEM LAPIDEM (on Jupiter the Stone) to promise adherence to the so concluded contract.

Roman denarius, c. 222 AD.
Emperor Severus Alexander left with a laurel wreath.
On the right Jupiter with sceptre and lightning thrower

Breaking the oath meant delivering oneself to the punishment of Jupiter. An animal sacrifice to the god underlined the seriousness of the vow.

- Prior to all state decisions, the Augurs had to obtain the opinion of Jupiter. The augury had been taken over from the Etruscans, though it significantly changed in Rome.

    The will of the god could be read by observation the flight of birds or from lightnings. According to the legend, already Romulus is said to have been enthroned by the appearance of eagles legitimating his rule.

    As the augurs kept their interpretation rules extremely secret and no one could understand how it had come to this or that result, they were also often suspected to have manipulated in a direction they wished (Livy, History of Rome, VI, 41).

    From the imperial era, therefore often astrologers were engaged who advised the ruling with respect to the outcome of their endeavors.

In addition to the augurs there were the HARUSPICES, who explored the will of different deities with the help of entrails; in this technique also taken over from the Etruscans there was particularly the state of the liver of the respective sacrificial animal of great importance, a practice that was used already by Babylonians and Greeks.

The above listing shows that in the Roman Empire Jupiter has to be seen in both the government and the private sector as a permanent presence. His rule was expressed by the ubiquitous practice of sacrifice. No important commitment was made without assurance of its guarantor. In the triumphal processions he was celebrated as initiator and winner of the extension of the imperial territory.

Jupiter in Astrology

The astrological Jupiter rules Sagittarius, the sign before winter solstice. Then the sun moves to its lowest point. This encourages the use of this time to think about what the past year has brought. Such considerations may lead to the well known Autumn depression or lay the foundations for New Year's resolutions.

In current western astrology Jupiter is ranked among the so-called social planets, planet symbols, which describe less the individual aspects of a personality, but more the embedding of the horoscope owner into a social structure.

The associated symbol ♃ is explained by Gertrud Hürlimann as a combination of a waxing moon over the cross of matter. In mundane astrology the moon symbolizes the people, the accumulation of humans living together. The glyph thus expresses mental increase (raising the subject from matter) in the context of the fellow human beings.

This increase can present itself as social structuring: Political organization, jurisdiction, ethical norms, a social structure in which everybody can arrange himself, without being restricted; all these are more than only an accumulation of humans. A given constitution allows each person their own place in the social order. Without such structures, nobody can rely on others, a human co-existence is inconceivable.

This seems self-evident in today's western democracies. Even protesters against government actions have confidence that they can exert their right to demonstrate, that everything runs according to legal rules and that they can call a court in case of doubt, if ever they believe that their rights had been restricted. The social order is relied on even where it is questioned.

Among the Babylonians, Jupiter was considered "Star of the King", what was seen in the report about the magi who are said to have come to the birth of Jesus. It is the largest planet of our solar system and reflects so much light that it is visible as a bright star in the night sky. It is apparently the most important heavenly body.

Before the discovery and assignment of Neptune Jupiter also ruled the sign Pisces. Meanwhile, Astrologers have the opinion that particularly the boundlessness of this astrological Symbols does not fit to Jupiter.

This is reflected in European democratic state order. The jurisdiction which is symbolized by Jupiter has an important function in the evaluation of legitimacy, in practice it stands above government and legislative institutions. The constitutional courts up to the European Court can condemn the actions of the rulers, and thus force them to modify or to renew them. This role of the legislature is historically unique, because until the introduction of modern democratic rules the respective ruler, king, emperor, or czar stood above the law.

The king in monarchy is however symbolized by the sun in modern Astrology, as well as the respective government in republics. They are indeed associated with the main star in the solar system, but the law that they are subjected to, is described in its importance by the Jupiter symbol.

The structure of good social order, which guarantees everybody best possible realization of his personal aptitudes, is symbolized by Jupiter.

> Embedding in a reliable social system enables the
> development of personality.

Social security allows development, exploration of one's own possibilities and their elaboration. Such expansion exceeds the existing limits.

This can take place immaterially in form of increasing scientific knowledge. Here, the difference to the Mercury symbol is clear to see: While in the Mercury symbol basic techniques and skills such as reading, writing, and communicating are concerned, Jupiter symbolizes higher education, religious connection to a superior being, philosophy and more generally the development of mankind through knowledge.

The physical crossing of borders is included in the Jupiter symbol as well. Although today in Central Europe expeditions into the wilderness belong to the past, many people individually contact the world "beyond the borders" in many ways via the media and explore it personally by travelling abroad.

In a negative exaggeration, border crossings at the expense of others appear in the interpersonal sphere as arrogance, on interstate level as imperialism. Rampant expansion in the physical area is experienced as a cancer.

The concrete interpretation tags are listed in the "Lexikon der astrologischen Zuordnungen", where 2063 rulerships are specified to illustrate this abstract definition of the Jupiter symbol.

Summary

The considerations have shown clearly that the astrological Jupiter symbol coincides in many aspects with the significance of the Roman god Jupiter. Not the mythological stories about the Greek Zeus, but the NOMINA ACTIONIS (pp 75) of the supreme Roman god reflect sufficiently the content that can be seen.

Propagation and expansion in legality and regularity are the basic tenor of both the Roman Jupiter, who promoted the spread and expansion of the Roman Empire under his reign, as well as the astrological symbol, which indicates the possibility of further development on the basis of a social order in the horoscope.

But the astrological Jupiter symbol is also a good illustration of the dangers which arise from unrestrained expansion and unregulated broadening of any kind.

In the Middle Ages the astrological Jupiter principle was considered as "great luck" (added by Venus, the "little luck"). Today in the individual horoscope it is interpreted rather as a way to develop the personality and self-realization.

A comparison with the American "The Rulership Book" shows, that the respective organization of government and law 'shines through'. Here an example: A juror in a German court is a lay judge, with the same duties and rights as a judge; the astrological signature of this activity is the Jupiter symbol. In contrast jurors (the jury) in American legal system represent the voice of the people and therefore are assigned to the astrological symbol moon.

Nowadays, politicians and representatives of social institutions are expected to perform impeccably; their lives are eamined down to their youth and former misdeeds are mercilessly brought to the public arena. In this way they are made to virtual successors of the FLAMEN DIALIS.

Some rulerships of the planet symbol Jupiter as facet model

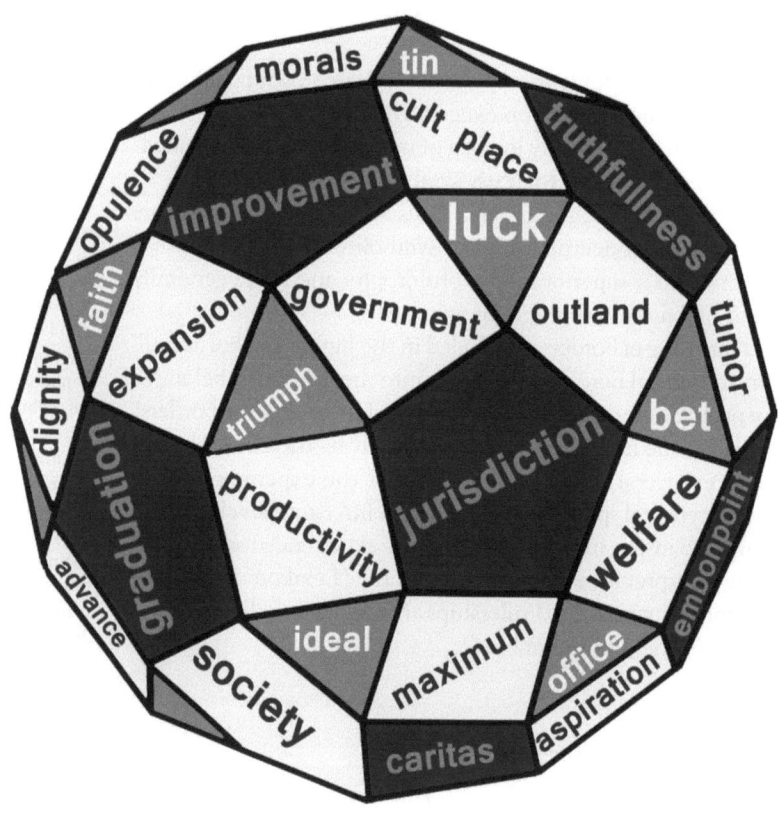

This section is based in particular on the following literature, where further information can be found:

Alföldi, Andreas, Das frühe Rom und die Latiner, Darmstadt 1977.

Hürlimann, Gertrud I., Astrologie, Zürich 1987.

Kerenyi, Karl, Die Religion der Griechen und Römer, München 1963.

Müller, Volker, Römische Religionsgeschichte, Universität München, Fachdidaktik klassische Philosophie, WS 2010-11.pdf

Saturn

Prehistory

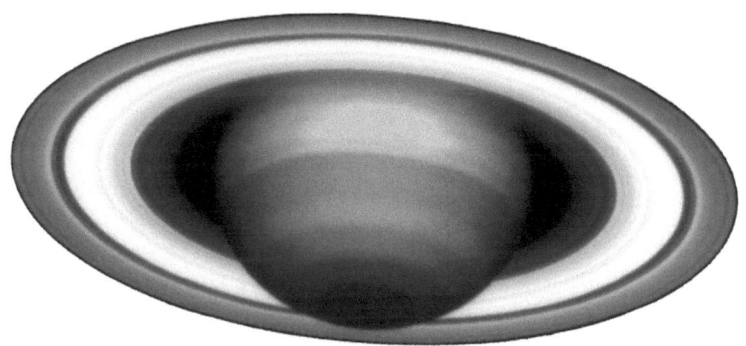

Saturn with his characteristic rings is often photographed

The outermost planet of our solar system, visible to the naked eye, was called in Sumerian udu.idím–sag–uš, in Babylonian genna and in Akkadian kajjàmànu "regularly". Up to the 14th century BC it was the star of the underworld god Nergal, tutelary god of the city of Kutha or Kuthu. Later the planet was associated to the god of war and hunting Ninurta who had his main temple in Nippur. The background of this exchange with the god of the planet Mars is unknown.

Although there are indications, that Uranus already was known among the Babylonians this knowledge was lost at least at the turn of the eras.

In some cuneiform documents it is also called "Star of the Sun", because according to the Babylonian doctrine of substitution, it represented the central light, when it had set. In its slow movement, it was considered an image of the Sun when it had become tired. Following v. Stuckrad, for the Mesopotamian priest astrologers Saturn represented justice, stability and order.

Up to the 18th century six planets (the Earth included) were taken into account.

Hor-ka-pet
Horus as celestial bull

1. New Kingdom

2. Ptolemaic time

The link between Saturn and Sun also corresponds to the Egyptian view that connected Saturn to hor–ka–pet, Horus as a celestial bull.

In Greece, Saturn became the star of the titan Cronus, ruler of the golden age, a quite contradictory mythological figure. On the one hand Cronus gained his power by castrating his father Uranus and exiling him to the sky – albeit at request of his mother Gaia. Because it had been predicted to him that he would also be destroyed by one of his children, he swallowed these right after their births. On the other hand, he was the peaceful ruler of the Golden Age, who lives ever now on the Isle of the Blessed.

Cronus' attribute is a sickle sword, which he received from his mother Gaia to castrate his father Uranus. Therefore SATURNUS was chosen as divine counterpart in the Roman pantheon, just because he also bears a sickle sword (harpe).

On the left Cronus, on the right
SATURNUS
both with head covered and Harpe.
The name Saturnus isn't mentioned
with this figure, it was derived only
from the attributes

SATURNUS as a Roman god

In the Roman tradition of sacred places, there was the **ARA**, a sort of table or votive stone, on which offerings were placed. Often, this was a place of worship under the open sky, which consisted only of this altar.

Buildings, where gods lived were called **AEDES**, they were at least partly covered, and often contained a statue of the deity and an altar.

TEMPLUM was a square designated to divination by augurs.

SATURNUS is one of the oldest Roman gods. Several different theories about his origin existed, today he is assumed to come from the Sabines.

The origin and meaning of his name is disputed; already in the Republican era its sense was lost. MARCUS TERENTIUS VARRO (s. p. 7) reports a (false) linguistical correlation with sowing in the 5th volume of his work "DE LINGUA LATINA": AB SATU EST DICTUS SATURNUS (after sowing he is called Saturnus). Varro spezifies Latium as his original dominion.

But even in the earliest days of Rome, there was a worship place of Saturn (ARA SATURNI) right next to the UMBILICIUS URBIS, the symbolic focal point of the imperium, from which the miles of all military roads were counted. The Capitoline Hill was said to have been MONS SATURNUS before it became centre of the town. Where ever you look, there are no serious traces of connection to agriculture.

By the year 500 BC, a temple (AEDES SATURNI) was built and renewed several times in the following centuries. The row of columns visible today dates from 283 AD, as well as the frieze and the inscription on it: "The

Preserved Column row of the antique Saturn temple

Senate and the people of Rome have rebuilt this temple after a fire". This is extraordinary because temple buildings usually were paid by rich citizens.

In this temple the AERARIUM POPULI ROMANI (treasure of the Roman people) was kept. It was also called AERARIUM SATURNI. In addition, in the Saturn temple the following items were stored separately each:

- The Sacred Treasure (AERARIUM SANCTUM), the emergency reserve;
- the standards of the legions;
- records of relevant laws on bronze plaques;
- copies of the decrees of the senate in books to look up (Original documents in the Ceres temple).

In addition, in the temple of Saturn the state mint was placed until it changed residence to the temple of IUNO MONETA (allegedly 289 BC).

The AERARIUM was managed by two Quaestors and stood under constant supervision of the Roman Senate. It consisted of precious metals, money, army standards, certificates and bonds.

At the same time it also served as an archive for public documents.

The AERARIUM was fed by taxes, revenues from leasing, fines and spoils of war.

Despite this outstanding importance in the public sector SATURNUS did not belong to the DEI CONSENTI, the twelve state gods. No special priest (FLAMEN) and no special college of priests was responsible for his cult, at least there are no sources that report information about this point of his veneration. In inscriptions he is rarely mentioned, besides some listings along with other gods.

Only the ARGEI rituals and the SATURNALIA (see below) indicate that he is an important Roman god. Of course it could be possible that he was such a natural part of Roman common life, that nobody thought it necessary to write something about him.

The only (private) inscription found in Rome originated from a 'foreigner', a man belonging to the celtic Remi:

SATURNO M[ARTI] / IOVI / MER-CURIO / HERCULI // M(ARCUS) QUARTINIUS M(ARCI) F(ILIUS) CIVES SABINUS REMUS / MILES COH(ORTIS) VII PR(AETORIAE) ANTONINIAN(A)E V(INDICIS) P(IAE) V(OTUM) L(IBENS) S(OLVIT)	To Saturn, Mars, Jupiter, Mercury (and) Hercules has Marcus Sabinus, son of Marcus Quartinius, citizen Remi, man-at-arms of the VII. Anthonian Praetorian cohort for the victory his pious vow gladly redeemed.
	(Vatican museum)

After Saturn had been equated to the Greek titan Cronus, the king of the golden age, by the adoption of Greek 'culture', Roman Emperors entitled themselves "Saturnus Augustus", thus demonstrating their actions as rulers of peace.

Mythological remains

According to Flavius Josephus the Jewish Sabbath was officially respected in the Roman Empire up to 135 AD; this leads to the interpretation that Caesar equated Yahweh with Saturn when designating Saturday, the Jewish sabbath as DIES SATURNI.

The original significance of Saturn was already forgotten during the Republican period, at least, no records exist. Only the rituals described below remained, some of which were carried out painstakingly until the declaration of Christianity as the state religion. It was known that he 'always' resided at (or on) Capitol Hill and that his name occurs in the Salian Chant. The latter can not be verified because of this text only a few fragments have been preserved in which there is no apparent indication of SATURNUS. Some interesting mythological records are:

1. There are no COGNOMEN ACTIONIS (epithets of action) recorded, no concrete spheres, for which Saturnus could be responsible.

2. The original place of worship was right next to the UMBILICIUS URBIS, navel and centre of the city of Rome and at the same time (suspected) entrance to the "world under the earth".

3. Part of funeral rites were combats where slaves or prisoners of war had to fight to death at or before the tombs; the fighters were dedicated to Saturn. From this habit emerged the gladiatorial battles which became popular entertainment later (see below).

In those literary works, in which Saturn was equated with the Greek Cronus, the fertility goddess Ops, equivalent to Rhea, was regarded as his wife.

4. Along with Saturn a female (?) LUA was worshipped; the weapons of defeated enemies were sacrificed to her. Her name is associated by Dumézil with "destruction, dissolution, perdition". Since neither a place of worship nor any celebrations of her are known, the assumption exists, that similar to Mars' Nerio (see p. 58) LUA concerns a personalized aspect of Saturn himself.

5. In his temple there stood a cult image (made of wood, filled with oil), whose feet were tied with wool; the bonds were untied for the time of Saturnalia.

6. The cult image bore in its hand a so-called **harp** (Greek: ἅρπη), a sword with a sickle protrusion along one edge near the tip of the blade. This is a weapon that also appears as the insignia of the Pharaoh in Egyptian reliefs. Perhaps this ruler symbol has come to Saturn from the Etruscans, who indeed had contacts with Egypt.

Likewise the weapon of the Greek titan Cronus was not a **drepanon** (δρεπανο), a harvesting tool, but a **harp** (Greek ἅρπη), a sickle sword.

   Apparently this **harp** and its meaning was unknown in the Renaissance, so it became confounded with an harvesting tool, the sickle.

7. In front of the 'new' temple of 500 BC emperor Augustus erected a column, from which all distances in the Roman Empire were calculated; it was henceforth regarded as the 'navel' of the Roman Empire.

It was no longer known in historical times what NUMEN actually was called Saturn. The functions attributed to him can be composed or have something to do with his original divinity. The linguistic closeness of his name

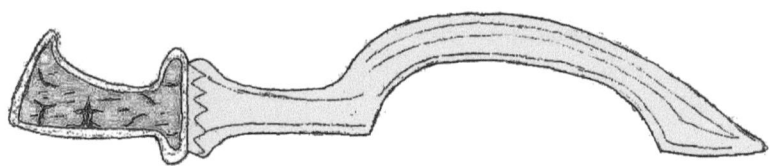

Modern drawing of a sickle sword

was the chief god of Carthage. He was a weather god considered responsible for the fertility of vegetation and esteemed as King of the Gods. Greco-Roman sources report that the Carthaginians burned their children as offerings to BA'al Hammon.

Statue of the Carthaginian god Ba'al Hammon in the Bardo Museum (Tunisia)

A typical **circular reasoning** regarding antique deities:

Saturnus was equated with Cronos because both had a sicle sword in their hands. Cronos swallowed his children. Children were offered to Ba'al Hammon by throwing them into his symbolic mouth. Thus Ba'al Hammon is equal Saturnus.

to the (classical) Latin word for seed and the dating of his festival at the end of the winter sowing seduced Roman and Greek writers of the 3rd and 2nd century BC to conclude, that Saturn is the one "who guides to sow", however not as agricultural NUMEN; he was interpreted to be the teacher, who brought agriculture to the Italics. Accordingly, his curved sword was seen as a farm tool.

By equating with the Greek Kronos, who also bears a sickle sword, a fictitious story was created, which describes Saturn as ruler of a Golden Age of the pre-Roman Italy.

Through the literal INTERPRETATIO ROMANA Saturn and Kronos became equivalent which brought the Cronus-content of "eating his children" into the sphere of Saturn. Subsequently a connection was laid to BA'al Hammon, to whom in Carthage traditionally children were offered as human sacrifice. There are some North African mentionings of Saturn in this sense from the Imperial period.

In 1971, a votive stone for Saturn was found during soil preparation work in Obergummer, municipality of S. Valentino in Campo. The place is located in the former province of RAETIA, today South Tyrol. The inscription time is estimated as 71–200 AD.

The inscription reads:

	Completed
D	D(EO)
SATVR	SATUR
NO P P	NO P(AGANI) P(AGI)
SCARE	SCARE
DRAN	DRAN
O [ ]	O(RUM)

Possible translation:
> (Dedicated) To the god **Saturn** from the pagan village Scare
> (inhabited) by **Drani**.   (Translation Hannelore Goos)

A rather obscure Saturn connection gives the "Sachsenchronik" (Saxon Chronicle) of Konrad Bothe from 1492. He describes a god **Krodo** in East-Westphalian Saxony, who was also called **Satar**. His statue is said to have been destroyed during the great Saxon wars of Charlemagne. For the origin of the god and his two very different names, various proposals are made:

- A Saturn altar as remnants of a camp of the Roman general Drusus acquired by the local Germans around the turning of the eras.
- Worship of Saturn as Cronus by Greek mercenaries at this altar, which led to the Germanic name Krodo.
- Import of a Cronus-worship by Germanic slaves or mercenaries from Greece.
- An original local Germanic god Krodo became enriched mythologically.

The city Bad Harzburg promotes Krodo in the town. In this context in 2007, a Krodo statue was erected at the entrance to the old castle, the Harzburg, like the illustration in the Saxon Chronicle.

But there exists no proof for one of these theories.

Some indications of the sphere of influence of Krodo exist: His attributes wheel, fish, buckets and waving coat (Wind) should also point to his connection to Saturn, and that is said why he was also called Satar. The Statue of Krodo-Satar with these attributes comes at least from the Renaissance but provides no evidence about the ancient Saturn.

Krodo-Satar in the
Saxon Chronicle

93

Howsoever, the origin of the Roman god SATURNUS is veiled by many interpretations and reinterpretations. Why he bears the (royal) harpe, cannot be explained. For the usual label "farmer god" no reliable evidence exists, all the more since his sacrificial rituals, ARGEI and SATURNALIA, in the oldest sources are described as festivals only in the town of Rome; in contrast to Mars, nothing of a peasant tradition has been handed down.

His closeness to the UMBILICIUS (entrance to the underworld), his task as guardian of the people's treasure and the relationship to funeral rituals can be regarded as indications that the Roman SATURNUS has been a chthonic deity, comparable to the later Greek Plutos. This corresponds with the little information we have, because in antiquity people avoided mentioning deities of underworld and death.

But such conclusions only can remain speculations.

Cult

Although their original meaning was no longer known, the Saturn rituals were performed to the letter also in the centuries of the Roman Empire although already at that time only speculations existed, as to what they might have served.

On March 16th–17th and May 14th–15th the ARGEI have been committed. The March celebrations consisted of atonement sacrifices at 27 shrines (SACRA ARGEORUM), which were located within the Servian Wall. It is reported that at every altar a man-sized straw puppet (SIMULACRUM) was consecrated to Saturn and placed there in order to clean the town of harmful fumes. They were named ARGEI, just like the whole ritual.

In May, the main celebrations took place. Under the leadership of the PONTIFEX MAXIMUS (chairman of the pontiffs) and the REX SACRORUM (priestly king of sacrifice) a solemn procession of all high priests, Vestal Virgines and praetors moved from station to station and took over the straw puppets in a prescripted ceremony. Then the procession went down to the Tiber onto the PONS SUBLICIUS where the figures were one by one rededicated to Saturn and thrown into the river by Vestal Virgins. The FLAMINICA DIALIS (wife of the highest Jupiter priest) went

Map of Rome with the PONS SUBLICIUS

in front as a mourner, with uncombed hair and without her usual jewellery. It is believed that the Argei were a succession of former ritual human sacrifice.

In December, the most famous celebrations in honour of Saturn were held, the SATURNALIA. Although they are already noted in the oldest cult calendars from the 6th century BC, this was not initially an extraordinary feast date. Up to the year 45 BC December 17th was a day which was marked in the calendar with EN, so no high day, but only a memorial to the inauguration of the Saturn temple.

ENDOITIO EXITIO NEFAS, shortened EN determines days with a sacrificial act in the morning and in the evening, in between normal business activities took place.

The morning sacrifice and the feast began with untying the woollen shackles of the god's statue. Following Versnel bound gods (i.e. their statues) are a widespread phenomenon in ancient religions. For this practice, he gives three explanations:

» A god should be prevented from leaving his sanctuary and the city;
» A god is dangerous and should be prevented from harming men;
» A god acts alternatly between rest (tied) and activity phases (untied).

Removing the shackles symbolizes in each case the start of the exceptional period, when Saturn reigns unbounded. The first public action was a sacrifice to him. It is not possible to determine which animal was sacrificed there and which priests performed the ceremony. In domestic Saturn celebrations a suckling pig is said to have been offered by the house father to the deity. It is assumed that accordingly the public sacrificial animals were boars. However, no evidence for that exists.

There is a parallel between the Roman SATURNALIA and the Kronía celebrated in Athens in honour of Cronus at the end of July or beginning of August.

This is also a festival with a social state of exception, but its function as a harvest feast is clear.

Only from the 3rd century BC there are reports about his sacrifice and that it was performed bareheaded. This is referred in literature as RITU GRECO (according to the Greek rite). Whether it was actual the adoption of a Greek ritual provision or the expression of the reversal of everything ordinary is discussed controversially. Saturn himself was told at that time to have his head covered, so the custom may also mean that humans must not approach him as equal – undisguised deities accordingly were worshipped with a covered head. Even the possibility that this form of worship dates back to prehistoric times, must be taken into consideration, because there are no earlier records.

In 49 BC Julius Ceasar plundered the AERARIUM SATURNI during his fight against the republic. It looks like a remediation that whilst his calendar reform the SATURNALIA became the status of public feasts (NP), expanded to three and later seven days. Since 45 BC the days from December 17th on were holidays, during which even the judiciary was suspended.

NEFAS PIACULUM (NP) marked calendar days on which public sacrifices were performed and which were as holidays off work.

Dice gamblers on a wall painting
in Pompeji

It is safe to assume that the celebrations described by Livy (s. p. 4) and Macrobius refer to the time from 45 BC on: No work and days off from school for the duration of the festivities.

They began with untying the shackles of wool and a sacrifice, followed by a sumptuous public meal in which the deity was present in the form of his effigy placed on a dining couch (LECTISTERNIUM).

The traditional outcry "IO SATURNALIA" was proclaimed at the end and that started the general festivities. All normality should be turned into the opposite: all work rested, schools and courts were closed, slaves dined sumptuously or were even hosted by their masters. Critics of the ruling authorities could be brought out freely. Dice game, normally banned ouside houses, now was allowed. People feasted on the streets under conditions that can be compared with the carnival today.

Also inside the houses sacrifices, feasts and rich banquets were held. A symbolic feast king (the king of fools) who was also called wine king was elected, which indicates the loose morals at the time. Gifts, particularly candles, were exchanged; this custom survived in the Christian festival of Christmas.

Gladiator fighting (MUNERA GLADIATORUM), which were allowed only on a few days in the year, took place especially on the seven days of the SATURNALIA. Initially these were simple duels on graves in honour of the respective dead person; later they were held ever more elaborate and magnificent in pompous arenas by the emperor himself. But the fighters remained dedicated to Saturn, and the performance was considered a culture succession of former human sacrifice among the intellectuals.

After the festival had been more and more secularized, the SATURNALIA were celebrated extensively in the cities of the provinces too.

The celebrations ended with another sacrifice and the fixing anew of the woollen fetters around the feet of the statue in the temple of Saturn.

Gladiator bottle
with a relief decoration:
Murmillo gives Thraex
the coup de grace.

Saturn in Astrology

For centuries the 6th planet of the solar system was considered as farthest, as knowledge of Uranus was lost. So, Saturn's orbit served as the boundary between the solar system and the rest of the cosmos. In the Saturn symbol, much of this delimiting function of Saturn is recognized.

Astrologically Saturn is considered to be the second social planet. It can be understood as quite contrary to Jupiter. The glyph ♄ consists of a cross (symbol for matter) above two half-circles – increasing and decreasing moon. The character is basically the reverse of ♃.

While Jupiter indicates expansion, Saturn marks borders. Social limits form a structure wherein someone can move around safely. Everything that happens within it is estimated and rewarded. As long as the individual follows the social rules, success and recognition are granted.

The astrological Saturn rules the sign Capricorn, the first Winter sign. Temperatures are now the lowest of the whole year, nature seems to be in hibernation.

Many plants and animals however, need this resting phase. In particular the trees of the temperate zone anchored it in their life cycle.

> Within social boundaries action can be safe
> with granted success.

While Jupiter-ruled crossing borders remains a gamble whether you reach overwhelming success or abysmal failure, the positive Saturnian development is characterized by voluntary adaptation, responding to the external conditions, striving after recognition in society thus resulting a probably slow but steady permanent ascent.

The view, Saturn being a 'misfortune planet' was common in the Middle Ages, and this is understandable: Looking at the existence of people in that time, we find that life was predetermined and specified in unimaginable ways.

At birth already one's social class was definite, automatically resulting in social status and wealth or poorness. Occupation and spouse were determined by the parents, later-born children in peasant and artisan families could not marry for lack of income. With the necessary assets you could optionally be a mercenary, nun, monk or priest. A change of location had to be allowed by the relevant sovereign.

A narrow life that nobody can really imagine nowadays.

The astrological symbol Saturn, however, indicates limitations that even go beyond the usual extent of life circumstances. That could concern crop failures, famine, war or epidemics. No wonder that Saturn was widely seen as a predictor of misfortune.

The positiv function of a social boundary in communication is shown by the example, that, if a child expresses its wish by saying, "I want," it has less success than asking "may I please".

In the Middle Ages the Saturn principle astrologically was called "the great misfortune" (supplemented by Mars, the "little evil").

Today in individual chart readings it is rather suggested to show a way to self-determination and character development.

In contrast, people in modern Western societies live freely in a way that was inconceivable in the Middle Ages. Today, anyone can
- choose a partner without intervention of parents,
- establish himself, where suits him best (in consideration of rules even in another country),
- travel where he wants,
- enter the profession, in which he is interested, regardless of the father's profession,
- decide his own lifestyle.

But this liberality can in individual cases turn over to negatives:
- Free partner choice leads to unrealistic expectations from a possible partner, so that at the end any relationship is felt to be of no avail.
- Freedom to establish residence causes the demand of unlimited mobility of employees by employers.
- Freedom of travel causes the modern mass tourism with its destructive effects on foreign cultures.
- Free choice of career can lead to permanent work discontent, with thoughts that the person could have chosen a better job.
- The own lifestyle can go as far as self-destruction.

Since the 2nd World War the number of unmarried living persons (singles) has increased constantly in the western industrial countries.

Investigations show for more than 40 years, that about half the young people do not remain in their originally chosen profession.

Involuntarily one is reminded of Cronus, the Lord of the Golden Age who rules an empire of wealth and peace, but devours his children. The positive achievements of modern life may destroy the happiness of the individual as well as the regulations and heteronomy of former centuries.

In medieval Alchemy the metal lead was associated with the planet Saturn. This is not only a heavy element, but also very toxic. Its associations were accordingly phlegm and from this resulting slowness. Nowadays we know that lead has a very positive quality: it shields against radiation.

Alchemistical meditation figure for Saturn from the year 1624

"Visit the interior of the earth and by rectification (purification by 7 times repeated distillation) you will find the hidden stone."

In modern words: "There are seven bridges to be crossed, seven years of darkness to survive, . . ." (Chris de Burgh)

The symbol Saturn as a limitation has thus not become invalid, even today a person can not unfold freely beyond measure; stability, structure, and focus on the essentials are premises. Outer limits are replaced by an inner insight, which is expressed in the Saturn principle.

Like Jupiter, it covers expansion and personal development within a social context. However, whereas the astrological Jupiter symbolizes the crossing of boundaries, Saturn marks the preservation and return to what is possible. This can be experienced as misfortune, as fatality, which restricts life when borders are crossed too far.

Thus, Jupiter and Saturn astrologically can be well considered as opponents, which are mutually dependent; hence for a socially successful and happy life, the two principles should be in balance. From this abstract definition, the nearly 2.800 rulerships of Saturn in the "Lexikon der astrologischen Zuordnungen" derive. Of course, the work also contains the traditional negative signatures. Even though much predetermination and oppression has ceased as described above, the restrictions imposed by misfortunes such as disease or natural disasters continue to exist.

And so, in mundane astrology those elements of interpretation are still dominating that see Saturn as an indicator of setback in the broadest sense. Also in horary astrology, this planetary symbol is regarded as a negative indicator.

Before the discovery and assignment of Uranus to Aquarius Saturn also ruled in this sign.

Meanwhile, astrologers are convinced that this astrological rulership no longer fits to Saturn, because the sign Aquarius symbolizes rather polarity than stability.

Summary

Since the character of the Roman god SATURNUS largely remains a mystery, it is difficult to determine whether there is a relationship between him and the current astrological symbol Saturn. Only his bonds correspond to those rulerships designating narrowing and limiting.

There are some parallels to the above mentioned meaning by V. Stuckrad of Saturn in Mesopotamia (see p. 87) and the Greek myths about Cronus. The latter can be obviously used best to illustrate the Saturn symbol. However, it should be noted that the respective myths of the Roman writers are rather poetic inventions like Saturnus as ruler of a golden age in Italy. It is quite possible that this fiction contains aspects of the god, yet they should not be considered to be religious writings.

The tension between a defined order and self-realization, earned luck and undeserved misfortune, development and persistence, remains encrypted in the the astrological Saturn symbol and is seen as everyone's life's work in each horoscope.

Some rulerships of the planet symbol Saturn as facet model

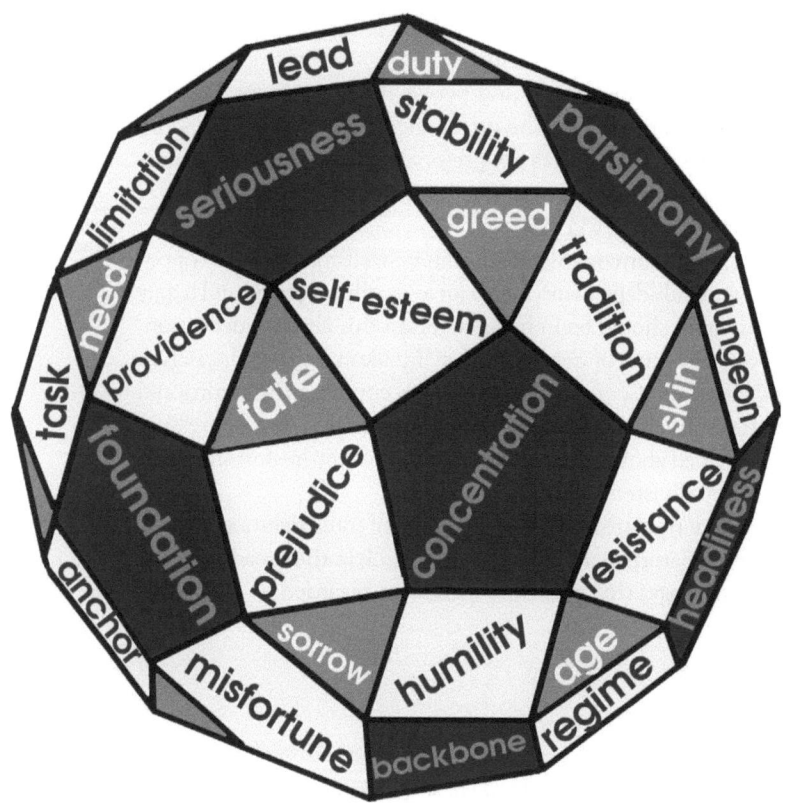

This section is based in particular on the following literature, where further information can be found:

Greene, Liz, Saturn, New York (USA), 1976.

Hürlimann, Gertrud I., Astrologie, Zürich (CH), 1987.

Muth, Robert, Einführung in die griechische und römische Religion, 2. Auflage, Darmstadt 1998.

Versnel, H. S., Inconsistencies in Greek and Roman Religion II, Leiden (NL) 1994.

Concluding Comments

At the beginning of the study presented here, the issue was raised of the mythological background of the Roman gods. The result:

There is none! Without mythology, without divine families and without a creation myth the Roman religion turns out to be completely different from any other Indo-European belief system.

The Roman PIETAS (piety) is expressed by the meticulous observance of ritual rules, both in the home and in the public area. The rituals were partly performed until the introduction of Christianity, when the knowledge about their importance was already lost for centuries. It is only indirectly possible to deduce the meanings of the Roman gods through the customs recorded in the festival calendars; even this, as shown by Saturn, is not possible in all cases.

Romans like Cicero were quite proud of the 'sobriety' of their religion, but in fact it did not seem to satisfy the religious needs of most people. So Etruscan architects and sculptors were already in pre-republican times commissioned to build temples and create statues showing the originally bodyless Roman gods. This craftsmen's work was based on Greek models. So Greek and Roman deities seem early to demonstrate an apparent connection. The takeover of ecstatic cults such as the MAGNA MATER (Cybele) and Isis suggests that there was quite a need for emotional attachment to divine entities. But this did not affect the original cults of the Roman gods.

The last Etruscan king, Tarquinius Superbus, is said to have brought the Sibylline Books to Rome. This is a collection of oracles, originally of Greek origin. In situations of need and state crisis they were consulted. They show a source of Greek influence on Roman civilisation, in particular by introducing an Apollo-cult and the rites of LECTISTERNIA. If this had an influence on the established Roman PIETAS can't be determined.

Due to increasing cultural exchange with the Greek towns south of Rome and after the 2nd invasion of Macedonia (200–197 BC), the Roman intellectuals came into contact with Greek literature, drama poetry and mythology. This was enthusiastically received by them, translated into Latin and incorporated into various literary works. Writers such as Ovid and Virgil gladly used Greek myths in their poetic fiction and developed them further adjusted to Italic conditions. However, bear in mind that literature in our sense was accessible only to a very small group of intellectuals. Books had to be handwritten on parchment and carefully reproduced in only a few copies. The main publishing took place via declamations by poets during festivities, but these festivals usually were performed to closed companies of certain patrician families or colleges. For the official religious cult and the popular piety, this had no effect.

Legends of gods existed in the aerea that became Rome.

Vesta and **Vulcan** are suspected to be related to an original creation from fire.

These stories are said to be suppressed by the Romans themselves. (Muth, p. 215)

The name MAGNA GRAECIA, English: Great Greece, denominated Greek settlements, which were founded by Greek colonists from the 8th century BC on in Sicily and in the south of the Italian mainland up to the region of modern Naples.

Unfortunately, classical scholarship from the Renaissance period up to the beginning of the 20th century viewed Roman literature as a source for the Roman religion. Consequently, their descriptions of a Roman Pantheon almost became a replica of the Greek one, including a confusion of Greek and Roman deities. This approach still can be found in popular literature about the gods of Greeks and Romans, and especially in pseudo-scientific descriptions on the Internet.

One of the most wide-spread and popular Books was "Gustav Schwab's Myths of Greece and Rome". Gustav Benjamin Schwab (1792–1850) was a German writer, pastor and publisher. Schwab's collection of myths and legends of Antiquity, published from 1838 to 1840, was widely used at German schools and became very influential for the reception of classical Antiquity in German classrooms.

In the field of serious religious studies this sight was continuously given up since the beginning of the 20th century (Wissowa, Kerenyi, Latte, etc.). Therefore, attempts have been made in this book to refer to the most recent literature, even if the respected article only deals with some aspects and is not published in English. In any case, the given descriptions should have made visible the characteristics of the respective Roman deities according current views.

Compared with the astrological symbols of the same name it is noticeable first, how strong a point of view depends on social conditions. The meaning of a central circumstance of existence such as luck – misfortune, wealth – poverty, love – hate, friendship – opposition and self-determination – suppression have changed much in the past 400 years. The life under a manorial lord, once absolutely common, would be felt nowadays as an intolerable suppression. Particularly the introduction of democratic state organisations, the absence of direct acts of war and in recent decades the change of family patterns have opened new sights and made earlier opinions no longer useful for astrological interpretation. The actual symbols naturally didn't change, only the perspective on them is new. The core of the interpretation of planetary constellations is, as V. Stuckrad writes, applicable for more than 3000 years invariable.

The rapid development of natural sciences has not only made major changes in the area of technology and the production of goods, but through the development of well functioning contraceptives enabled the revolution of sexual morality and reproductive behaviour.

The starting point of the considerations was the question, how far Roman conceptions of deities agree with the contents of the astrological symbols that are named after them. This includes quite a distinction from Greek mythology, although in many astrological papers Greek myths are used as being constituent a for the respective planet symbol.

Likewise, the Jungian concept of archetypes is mentioned but not pursued. No mythological background could be found to allow that way of explanation. Jung seems to have based his considerations on Greek myths as most of his contemporaries did.

Yet, the astrological understanding of the meaning of the symbols is the only way to understand the connection between the respective Roman deity and its interpretation in an astrological chart. This point of view also allows comparisons and continuation towards current private and social problems that play a role in astrological consultation.

Detailed considerations of the investigation results are presented in the chapter on the respective deities. In summary, however:

- The astrological **Mercury symbol** largely contains the ruler-ships representing the Roman ideas of their god Mercury. He embodies action even in a figurative sense and communication on an equal level. This corresponds to the associated zodiac sign Gemini. The Greek Hermes is less represented, since his task as a Messenger of the gods is not communication of the same type and his function as psychopomp, a guide for the deceased to the underworld, is not included in the symbol of the planet Mercury.

- The **Venus symbol** can be deduced very well from Roman ideas of Venus, in particular, the fact that the Roman Venus occurs in two forms, as a mediator of legal relations, and as the goddess of (autonomous) female sexuality. This corresponds well with the current views of the astrological symbol of Venus, which reigns in the zodiac sign Taurus, as well as in Libra. The content of the Greek myths of Aphrodite are less represented by the astrological symbol, especially as they are often reduced to narratives of self love and promiscuity.

- The perception of the **Mars symbol** had to change remarkably in the absence of wars conducted by the Western industrial nations since the 2nd World War. Henceforth the people of these countries are not directly affected by the events of war, even though there are still wars in many parts of the world. Here the Roman ideas of a god who protects the boundaries outwardly, guards against dangers and supports just wars by active fighting, meets the current importance.

    The assignment to the zodiac sign Aries also indicates a relationship of the Mars principle to modern popular sports, which may be an active use of martian energy. Already in Roman times people mocked at the 'mindless' berserker-like Ares from Greek mythology, his appearance today thus describes a negative or even pathological facet of the Mars symbol.

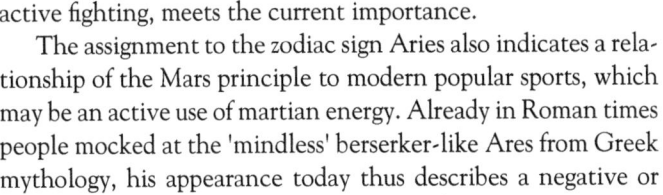

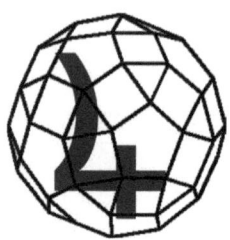

- The **Jupiter symbol** is the best in line with Roman ideas of the supreme god. Jupiter was the guarantor of the spread of the Roman Empire, which according to the ideas of the Romans brought system, culture and justice to the barbarians. It is the epitome of the astrological Jupiter symbol today to show comparable assignments to social order structures and the possibility of the unfolding of the individual in these. The shifting of boundaries that took place in the Roman Empire under the reign of Jupiter, is now realized as a freedom of movement and right of travel to almost every region in the world. Of the Greek Zeus described in popular literature mainly as an active fighter against the titans and conqueror of various women, nothing is left in today's astrological Jupiter symbol.

- The **Saturn symbol** cannot be compared with the Roman ideas about their god Saturnus because hardly anything is known of him. The existing evidence points to a chtonic deity whose domain deals with both bondage and guarding of (subterranean?) treasures.

  Here the mythological tales about the Greek titan Cronus fit better. They illustrate how a king of peace, ruler of the Golden Age, at the same time becomes the devourer of his children, who nevertheless finally bring the end of his reign. Already the Sumerians are said to have symbolized order and justice in their deity equivalent to Saturn and positive social principles. But in excess, these Saturnian virtues actually can 'devour their children' if order becomes dictatorship or if the private economy turns to avarice.

Among others an intriguing fundamental question remains unresolved at the end: Why, in the transition from one pantheon to another, certain gods are chosen as equivalents of the previous representatives of a planetary symbol while others are not? There is not one rationally justifiable response. Notions of divine beings may be enclosed with in the unconscious and come to fruition in time of such a selection. And thus, the historical series of the gods associated with planetary symbols can only be accepted and the available knowledge about these gods used to understand more, in order to improve astrological knowledge.

Dear Reader,

this book is a translation of the German "Götter am Himmel", published in 2014. I hope you enjoyed reading it.
If you have questions concerning the content, don't hesitate to ask me.

Undoubtedly, you have noticed mistakes in grammar and phrasing; the latter sometimes even may be a bit archaic. The main reason for that is, that German is my mother tongue and the original German book was translated using my more than 50 years old school English. With the voluntary help of Joanna Gibson and my Dutch husband this edition was realised.

Based on the modern times of various ways of electronic interaction, you, dear reader, are wholeheartedly invited to contribute to a revised edition by sending me your grammar corrections, proposals for better phrasing, etc.

Please send your remarks to: HGoos@Sonnenastro.de
Or contact me in a PM through my husband's Facebook account at:
https://www.facebook.com/GardenStone

No doubt, together we will be able to get an improved edition in better, more commonly used English!

And, as a matter of course, your highly appreciated help will be expressed by mentioning your name at the 'thanks' page, which will replace this page in the next edition (of course only if you agree).

Thanking you in advance,
Hannelore Goos

Illustrations

P. 3   Quelle: http://ancientrome.ru/art/artworken/img.htm?id=72 ©Istituto Geografico De Agostini S.p.A. — Novara

P. 4   https://upload.wikimedia.org/wikipedia/commons/d/df/Rome_in_753_BC.png, GNU

P. 9   http://commons.wikimedia.org/wiki/File:Lararium,_Pompeji.JPG, © Claus Ableiter, GNU.

P. 10   http://commons.wikimedia.org/wiki/File:Map_Forum_-_Temple_of_Concordia, Plan Rome 1916, © Joris, PD.

P. 11   http://commons.wikimedia.org/wiki/File:Forum_Portique_Dii_consentes.jpg?uselang=de, © Ursus, GNU.

P. 13   http://grosssteingraeber.de/seiten/schweden/skane/ales-stenar.php, with kind permission of Reinhard Möws

P. 14   http://commons.wikimedia.org/wiki/File:Cetus_constellation_map.png, © 2003 Torsten Bronger, GNU.

P. 15   http://www.bible-history.com/ibh/Assyrian+Customs/Treaty/, Bible History online,10.12.13.

P. 15   www.aina.org, Detail of Assurbanipal's standard inscription, People Of Ancient Assyria (Jorgen Laessoe).

P. 16   St. Gallen, Stiftsbibliothek, Cod. Sang. 902, http://www.e-codices.unifr.ch/de/list/one/csg/0902..

P. 19   http://commons.wikimedia.org/wiki/File:Mithrasrelief-Neuenheim.JPG, Badisches Landesmuseum Karlsruhe, ©Thomas Ihle, GNU.

P. 19   http://commons.wikimedia.org/wiki/File:Dehio_1_Pantheon_Floor_plan.jpg, aus: Georg Dehio/Gustav von Bezold: Kirchliche Baukunst des Abendlandes. Stuttgart 1887-1901, Tafel 1, PD.

P. 20   http://commons.wikimedia.org/wiki/File:3K%C3%B6nige,RavennaGe%C2%B9%C2%B375%C2%B0.jpg, © Geofreda Geoffrey, GNU.

P. 25   http://totallyfreeimages.com/56/Nebo, Seven Great Monarchies Of The Ancient Eastern World, Vol 1, PD

P. 25   http://de.wikipedia.org/wiki/Sebeg

P. 26   http://munzeo.com/coin/helios-herennius-etruscus-antoninian-rom-5242297

P. 28   Putzger, Historischer Weltatlas, Berlin 1978, p. 10 (snippet).

P. 29   http://commons.wikimedia.org/wiki/File:Mercury_%28deity%29_relief.jpg?uselang=de, © Ad Meskens, GNU.

P. 31   http://www.academic.ru/dic.nsf/meyers/90356/Merkur.

P. 34   http://commons.wikimedia.org/wiki/File:Gripswalder-Matronenstein-Mercurius-_Arvernus-01.png, PD.

P. 39   http://upload.wikimedia.org/wikipedia/commons/6/63/Puppenbruecke_01.JPG, © Traumrune / CC-BY-3.0

P. 41   http://commons.wikimedia.org/wiki/File:Ishtar_Eshnunna_Louvre_AO12456.jpg, © Marie-Lan Nguyen, CC.

P. 41   http://de.wikipedia.org/wiki/Netjer-duai.

P. 43   http://commons.wikimedia.org/wiki/File:Altar_twelve_gods_Louvre_Ma666.jpg, © Marie-Lan Nguyen, CC.

P. 44   http://upload.wikimedia.org/wikipedia/commons/d/d6/Colonne_Tempio_Venere_Colosseo_Roma_09feb08.jpg?uselang=de, © Marcok - it.wikipedia.org, CC.

P. 45   http://de.dreamstime.com/lizenzfreie-stockfotografie-pompeji-katholisch-fresko-image10894717.

P. 45   http://de.wikipedia.org/wiki/Datei:WLANL_-_Pachango_-_Allard_Pierson_-_Bronzen_Etruskische_wierrook-brander.jpg, Allard Pierson Museum, © Niels Pachango, CC.

P. 47   http://de.wikipedia.org/wiki/Datei:0_V%C3%A9nus_de_l%27Esquilin_-_Musei_Capitolini_-_Rome.JPG, © Jean-Pol GRANDMONT, CC.

P. 48   http://en.wikipedia.org/wiki/File:Fasti_Praenestini_Massimo_n2.jpg, National Museum of Rome, © Marie-Lan Nguyen / CC-BY 2.5

P. 51   http://de.wikipedia.org/w/index.php?title=Datei:R%C3%B6mische_Venus.JPG, © Hermann Junghans, GNU

P. 55   http://templeofninurta.weebly.com/ninurta.html

P. 55   http://www.britannica.com/EBchecked/media/29690/Nergal-a-Mesopotamian-god-of-the-underworld-holding-his-lion, Ashmolean Museum, Oxford, Eng.

P. 55   Putzger, Historischer Weltatlas, Berlin 1978, p. 5 below (snippet).

P. 56   http://de.wikipedia.org/wiki/Roter_Horus

P. 58   http://brf.be/nachrichten/international/153117.

P. 59   LVR-Archäologischer Park Xanten, LVR-Römermuseum.

P. 60   http://etc.usf.edu/clipart/15800/15837/ancile_15837.htm (snippet).

P. 60   Budge, Wallis E. A., An Account of the Roman Antiquities, London, 1907, p. 239.

P. 61   http://etc.usf.edu/clipart/15800/15837/ancile_15837.htm.

P. 62   http://commons.wikimedia.org/wiki/File:R%C3%B6misches_Horn_Slg_Ebn%C3%B6ther.jpg, Helvetiker, PD.

P. 63   http://de.wikipedia.org/wiki/Datei:Suovetaurile_Louvre.jpg, © Marie-Lan Nguyen (Januar 2005), CC.

P. 64   http://pixabay.com/de/wolf-tier-biologie-eckzahn-153807/, PD.

p. 67   https://commons.wikimedia.org/wiki/File:Mars_Ultor.JPG.

P. 69   http://upload.wikimedia.org/wikipedia/commons/4/4f/Marduk_and_pet.jpg, PD;

P. 69   http://de.wikipedia.org/wiki/Hor-wepesch-taui.

P. 70   http://commons.wikimedia.org/wiki/File:Mineral_S%C3%ADlex_GDFL104.jpg, © L. M. Bugallo Sánchez, GNU.

P. 71   http://en.wikipedia.org/wiki/File:Design_for_a_Stained_Glass_Window_with_Terminus,_by_Hans_Holbein_the_
         Younger.jpg, wikidata:Q48319, PD.

P. 72   History of Rome by Victor Duruy (Kegan Paul, Trench & Co, 1884).

P. 73   http://en.wikipedia.org/wiki/File:Monte_Cavo_e_lago_Albano.jpg, PD.

P. 78   http://de.wikipedia.org/wiki/Datei:Marduks_strid_med_Tiamat.jpg, PD.

P. 78   http://en.wikipedia.org/wiki/File:Flamen_Louvre_Ma431.jpg, © Marie-Lan Nguyen (2006), CC.

P. 79   http://en.wikipedia.org/wiki/File:Roman-calendar.png, PD.

P. 81   http://upload.wikimedia.org/wikipedia/commons/0/05/Grapes_02_pushkin.jpg, © shakko, CC.

P. 83   http://commons.wikimedia.org/wiki/File:ALEXANDER_SEVERUS_RIC_IV_5-824447_IOVIS.jpg, Quelle
         http://www.cngcoins.com/Coin.aspx?CoinID=131119, Urheber CNG, CC.

P. 87   http://commons.wikimedia.org/wiki/File:Saturn_-_Lord_of_the_Rings.jpg, Quelle:http://www.eso.org/gallery/v/
         ESOPIA/SolarSystem/phot-04a-02.tif.html, CC.

P. 87   http://de.wikipedia.org/wiki/Hor-ka-pet

P. 88   http://commons.wikimedia.org/wiki/File:Saturnus_fig274.png, Dr. Vollmers Wörterbuch der Mythologie aller
         Völker, third edition Stuttgart 1874, p. 406-407, PD.

P. 88   http://commons.wikimedia.org/wiki/File:0_Autel_d%C3%A9di%C3%A9_au_dieu_Malakb%C3%AAl_et_aux_
         dieux_de_Palmyra_-_Musei_Capitolini_%281b%29.JPG, © Jean-Pol GRANDMONT (2011), CC.

P. 89   http://upload.wikimedia.org/wikipedia/commons/9/9a/Temple_of_Saturn%2C_Rome.jpg, © Diana Ringo, CC.

P. 91   http://commons.wikimedia.org/wiki/File:Hopesh_Tyb_8_C.jpg, © MittlererWeg, CC.

P. 92   http://en.wikipedia.org/wiki/File:Baal_Hamon_Bardo.JPG, Bardo Museum in Tunisia, © Abalg, CC.

P. 92   http://www.gemeinde.karneid.bz.it/system/web/zusatzseite.aspx?detailonr=220736324.

P. 93   Bothe, Konrad, Die Cronecken der Sassen or »Sachsenchronik«, 1492, p. 32.

P. 94   http://upload.wikimedia.org/wikipedia/commons/d/d8/Plan_Rome_-_Pons_Sublicius.png, © Joris1919, CC.

P. 96   http://en.wikipedia.org/wiki/File:Pompeii_-_Osteria_della_Via_di_Mercurio_-_Dice_Players.jpg, © Manfred
         Rieger, CC.

P. 96   http://commons.wikimedia.org/wiki/File:GladiatorFeldflasche.jpg, Römisch-germanisches Museum, Köln, © BS
         Thurner Hof, CC.

Literature

General information source:
Das neue Taschenlexikon, Bertelsmann Lexikon Verlag, Gütersloh 1992.

Albers, Jon, Das Marsfeld in: Jon Albers und Gerd Graßhoff und Michael Heinzelmann und Markus Wäfler, Das Marsfeld in Rom. Beiträge der Berner Tagung vom 23./24. November 2007, Bern 2008.

Aigner-Foresti, Luciana, Die Etrusker und das frühe Rom, 2. Auflage, Darmstadt 2009.

Albrecht, Michael von (Übers. u. Hrsg.), Ovid Metamorphosen, Lateinisch/Deutsch, Reclams Univ.-Bibliothek Nr. 1360.

Alföldi, Andreas, Das frühe Rom und die Latiner, Darmstadt 1977.

Bills, Rex, The Rulership Book, Tempe (Arizona, USA) 1991.

Blunck, Jürgen, Götter in Planeten und Monden, Frankfurt am Main 1987.

Bömer, Franz, Iuppiter und die römischen Weinfeste, Rhein. Museum für Philologie, Ausg. 1941, P. 30-58,Bad Orb, 1941.

Breyer, Gertraud, Etruskisches Sprachgut im Lateinischen unter Ausschluss des spezifisch onomastischen Bereiches, Leuven (Belgien) 1993.

Carter, Jesse Benedict, The Cognomina of the Goddess "Fortuna",Transactions and Proceedings of the American Philological Ass., Coverage: 1897-1972 (Vols. 28-103), P. 60-68, Published by The Johns Hopkins University Press

Corriere della Sera, Redazione Roma online, Dall'Etruria al Medioevo: con il radiocarbonio la Lupa capitolina è più giovane di 17 secoli, Rom 22.06.12.

Cuoco, Antonio, Phantastische römische Mythologie, Remda-Teichel 2015.

Damste, Dr. Onno, Romeinse Sagen en Verhalen, Utrecht (NL)/Antwerpen(BE) 1958.

Dickmann, Jens-Arne, Pompeji: Archäologie und Geschichte, München 2005.

Götter der Etrusker – Zwischen Himmel und Unterwelt (Sonderausstellung 14.10.2017 – 4.2.2018 im Archäologischen Museum Frankfurt) – Texte der Wandtafeln

Dietz, Otto Edzard (Hrsg.), Erich Ebeling (Autor), Bruno Meissner (Autor), Reallexikon der Assyriologie und Vorderasiatischen Archäologie, Bd. 3, Bd. 10, Berlin 1971, Berlin 2005.

Dietz, Otto Edzard, Geschichte Mesopotamiens von den Sumerern bis zu Alexander dem Großen, München 2004.

Döderlein, Ludwig, Handbuch der lateinischen Synonymik, Heidelberg 1871.

Dorcey, Peter F., The Cult of Silvanus, New York 1992.

Drosdowski, Günther, Das Herkunftswörterbuch, Duden Etymologie, Mannheim 1989.

Dumézil, Georges, Archaic Roman Religion, aus dem Französischen übersetzt von Philip Krapp, Baltimore 1996.

Eisenhut, Werner, Augures, in: Der Kleine Pauly (KlP), Band 1, Stuttgart 1964.

Fasching, Gerhard, Sternbilder und ihre Mythen, 3. erweiterte Auflage, Hamburg 2000.

Forsythe, Gary, A Critical History of Early Rome, London, 2005.

Friedlaender, Ludwig, Sittengeschichte Roms, Essen 2000.

Frobenius, Leo, Vom Kulturreich des Festlandes, Berlin 1923.

Fuhrmann, Manfred, Geschichte der römischen Literatur, Stuttgart 2005.

GardenStone, Germanischer Götterglaube, Norderstedt 2009.

GardenStone, Der Merkur-Wodan-Komplex, Norderstedt, 2012.

GardenStone, Die Rückkehr der Göttin Nehalennia, Norderstedt 2008.

GardenStone, Gods of the Germanic Peoples, From Roman Times to the Viking Age, Norderstedt 2014.

Gehlhar, Fritz, Wie der Mensch seinen Kosmos schuf, Berlin 1996.

Gerlach,Wolfgang (Hrsg.), Publius Ovidius Naso. FASTI. Festkalender Roms, München 1960.

Goos, Hannelore, Lexikon der astrologischen Zuordnungen, Bd. 1-5, Norderstedt 2018-2019.

Greene, Liz, Sasportas, Howard, Die inneren Planeten, München 1995.

Greene, Liz, Saturn, München 1981.

Graf, Fritz, Iuppiter in: Der Neue Pauly, Brill Online, 2013.

Hunger, Dr. Herbert, Lexikon der griechischen und römischen Mythologie, Wien 1953.

Hürlimann, Gertrud I., Astrologie, Zürich 1987.

Huschke, E., Die oskischen und sabellischen Sprachdenkmäler, in: Zeitschrift für vergleichende Sprachforschung, 6. Bd., P. 62-75, Göttingen 1857.

Jacques, François, Scheid, John, ROM und das Reich in der hohen Kaiserzeit, Hamburg 2008.

Josephus, Flavius, The Antiquities of the Jews, translated by William Whiston, Wikisource, http://en.wikisource.org/wiki/The_Antiquities_of_the_Jews (7.12.2013).

Kaster, Robert A. (Hrsg.), Macrobius: Saturnalia. 3 Bände, (Text und engl. Übersetzung), Cambridge (Mass./USA), 2011.

Kerenyi, Karl, Die Mythologie der Griechen, Bd. 1, Die Götter- und Menschheitsgeschichten, Ungekürzte Ausgabe vom November 1966, 23. Aufl., München 2003.

Kerenyi, Karl, Auf den Spuren des Mythos, München und Wien 1967.

Kerenyi, Karl, Die Religion der Griechen und Römer, München 1963.

Klausen, Rudolf Heinrich, Aeneas und die Penaten, Die italischen Volksreligionen unter dem Einfluss der griechischen, Band 2, Hamburg und Gotha 1840.

Klingner, Friedrich, Römische Geisteswelt, 5. Aufl., München 1965.

Köbler, Gerhard, Lateinisches Abkunfts- und Wirkungswörterbuch, 2. Auflage, 2009.

Kolb, Frank, Das antike Rom: Geschichte und Archäologie, München, 2007.

Laessoe, Jorgen, People Of Ancient Assyria, Translated from the Danish by F. P. Leigh-Browne, Published 1963 A.D., Assyrian International News Agency, Books Online, http://www.aina.org.

Latte, Kurt, Römische Religionsgeschichte, Handbuch der Altertumswissenschaft, Abt. 5, Teil 4, München 1976.

Lieven, Alexandra von, Grundriss des Laufes der Sterne – Das sogenannte Nutbuch, Kopenhagen 2007.

Lindsay, Jack, Origins of Astrology, London, 1972.

Lübke, Wilhelm, Grundriss der Kunstgeschichte, Band 1, Esslingen 1901.

Marchant, Jo, Die Entschlüsselung des Himmels, Berlin 2011.

Marcus Aurelius, römischer Kaiser, Übers. Gleichen-Russwurm, Alexander, Freiherr von, Selbstbetrachtungen, Projekt Gutenberg Nr. 15028, 2005.

Maternus von Cilano, D. Georg Christian, Ausführliche Abhandlung der römischen Alterthümer. Dritter Theil, herausgegeben von Georg Christian Adler, Hamburg 1776.

McCall, Henrietta, Mesopotamische Mythen, Stuttgart 1993.

Mertz, Bernd A., Das große Handbuch der Astrologie, Sonderausgabe, München 1999.

Momigliano, Arnaldo, Essays in Ancient and Modern Historiography, Chicago 2012.

Müller, Volker, Römische Religionsgeschichte,http://www.fachdidaktik.klassphil.uni-muenchen.de/studium_lehre/lehrverans/winter_1011/uebung_grundwissen/roem_religionsgeschi.pdf

Muth, Robert, Einführung in die griechische und römische Religion, 2. Auflage, Darmstadt 1998.

Perowne, Stewart, Römische Mythologie, Wiesbaden 1969.

Petersmann, Hubert, Zu einem altrömischen Opferritual, Rhein. Museum für Philologie, Ausg. 1973, 238-255, Bad Orb, 1973.

Prayon, Friedhelm, Die Etrusker, München 2010.

Preller, Ludwig, Römische Mythologie, Bd. I und II, Berlin 1881.

Putzger, F. W., Historischer Weltatlas, 99. Aufl., Berlin 1978.

Radke, Gerhard, Beobachtungen zu einigen der ältesten in Rom verehrten Gottheiten, in: Rheinisches Museum für Philologie, Ausg. 1992, P. 268-282,Bad Orb, 1992.

Radke, Gerhard, Zur Entwicklung der Gottesvorstellung und der Gottesverehrung in Rom, Darmstadt 1987.

Radke, Gerhard, Die Götter Altitaliens, Münster 1979.

Ranke, Leopold von, Römische Geschichte, Hamburg 2012.

Ranke-Graves, Robert von, Griechische Mythologie, Quellen und Deutung, Neuausgabe in einem Band, Hamburg 1984.

Romankiewicz, Brigitte, Spielfeld der Götter, C.G. Jungs Archetypenlehre und die Astrologie,Tübingen 2002.

Sandner, Donald, So möge mich das Böse in Scharen verlassen, Solothurn und Düsseldorf 1994.

Schäfer, Thomas, Bildersprache Astrologie, Wettiswil (CH) 1991.

Schäfer, Thomas, Vom Sternenkult zur Astrologie, Düsseldorf 1993.

Schmidt, Jens Uwe, Die schneeweißen Arme der Venus, Zur Homer-Imitation in Vergils Aeneis, Bielefeld 1994.

Schmidt, Peter Lebrecht, Naevius, in: Der Kleine Pauly (KlP), Band 3, Stuttgart 1969.

Skeat, William W., Etymological Dictionary of the English Language, New York 2011 (first ed. 1882).

Steuding, Hermann, Mercurius, in: Wilhelm Heinrich Roscher (Hrsg.): Ausführliches Lexikon der griechischen und römischen Mythologie, Leipzig 1897.

Stiehle, Reinhardt, Wallrath, Bertram (Hrsg.), Eine literarische Astrologie,Tübingen, 2004.

Stuckrad, Kocku von, Geschichte der Astrologie, 2. überarbeitete Auflage, München 2007.

Ulf, Christoph, Das römische Lupercalienfest. Ein Modellfall für Methodenprobleme in der Altertumswissenschaft, Darmstadt 1982.

Varro, Marcus Terentius, DE LINGUA LATINA, LIBER V , http://www.thelatinlibrary.com.

Versnel, H. P., Inconsistencies in Greek and Roman Religion II, Leiden 1994.

Wagenvoort, Hendrik, The Origins of the Goddess Venus, in: Pietas, Leiden (NL) 1980.

Walter, Jörg, Entschlüsselte Aspektfiguren, Freiburg 1981.

Wifstrand-Schiebe, Marianne, Lactanz, Varro und die Tradition des Argeer-Ritus, in: Rheinisches Museum für Philologie, Heft 142, P. 189-209, Frankfurt am Main 1999.

Wissowa, Georg, Religion und Kultus der Römer, München 1902.

Wolf, Robert H. W. Mysterium Wasser: Eine Religionsgeschichte zum Wasser in Antike und Christentum, Göttingen 2004.

Wurm, Julius Friedrich, (Übersetzer), Diodor's von Sizilien historische Bibliothek, Stuttgart 1831.

Zobel, Hans-Jürgen, Göttertriaden im Alten Vorderen Orient und die alttestamentarische Gottesvorstellung in Altes Testament – Literatursammlung und Heilige Schrift S.137-154, Berlin 1993.

Internet sources

General information source:
      http://www.wikipedia.org (German, English, Dutch, French, Italien)

Webpages with date of visit (format DD-MM-JJJJ)

19-12-2012 http://www.neunplaneten.de/nineplanets/days.html

19-12-2012 http://cura.free.fr/decem/10kengil.html

19-12-2012 http://universal_lexikon.deacademic.com/257495/Jupiter,_Janus_und_Herkules_-_Alte_und_
neue_G%C3%B6tter_der_R%C3%B6mer

16-01-2013 http://www.wibilex.de/nc/wibilex/das-bibellexikon/details/quelle/WIBI/referenz/10254/cache/cac-
f81099ee07ecf086cac2ab5137b2e/

23-01-2013 http://www.stiftergym.at/thiel/noricum/badekult.php?thema=RELIGION&unterthema=12&raum=5&vitrine
=10&regal=11&titel2=12&count=0&s=&kapitel=not&zahl=&a=&help1=&aa=

04-02-2013 http://www.bible-history.com/ibh/Assyrian+Customs/Treaty/

04-02-2013 http://www.aina.org/books/poaa/poaa.htm#23

10-02-2013 http://www.e-codices.unifr.ch/de/list/one/csg/0902

                http://12koerbe.de/arche/aratos.htm

                http://www.bibelwissenschaft.de/nc/wibilex/das-bibellexikon/details/quelle/WIBI/zeichen/t/referenz/32270/
cache/e3dfda5f7d460d70729f0dd537e24ce5/

11-02-2013 http://www.gutenberg.org/ebooks/15028

13-02-2012 http://www.jstor.org/discover/10.2307/637186?uid=3737864&uid=2129&uid=2&uid=70&uid=4&s
id=21101802490627

17-02-2013   http://amor.cms.hu-berlin.de/~ossendrm/babylon08-ossendrijver.pdf

21-02-2013 http://www.wortmagier.de/img/werk/1/2.pdf

                http://www.pm-magazin.de/a/die-macht-der-symbole

                http://www.freimaurer-loge.de/symbole.html

                http://www.bpb.de/apuz/29747/die-macht-der-symbole?p=all

                http://www.amo-international.net/downloads/newsletter/newsletter35.pdf

22-02-2013 http://home.comcast.net/~chris.s/myth.html

                http://www.chemeurope.com/en/encyclopedia/History_of_astrology.html

26-02-13   http://www.nzz.ch/aktuell/startseite/kaiseraugst-merkur-inschrift-archaeologie-aargau-1.1141812#

                http://www.imperium-romanum.info/wiki/index.php?title=Mercurius

27-02-2013 http://www.reppa.de/lex.asp?ordner=m&link=Mars.htm

03-03-2013 http://ancientlinks.blogspot.de/search?q=Venus

                http://romanpagan.blogspot.com.au/2013/01/venus-goddess-of-love-and-life.html

05-03-2013 http://www.meritneith.de/astronomie.htm

                http://www.liebewohl.de/inhalt/liebesgottheiten.htm#hathor

06-03-2013 http://www.uni-protokolle.de/Lexikon/Venus_%28Mythologie%29.html

                http://ancientlinks.blogspot.de/search?q=Venus

                http://romanpagan.blogspot.com.au/2013/01/venus-goddess-of-love-and-life.html

                http://www.oxfordreference.com/search?q=Caere

06-03-2013 http://www.schreiben10.com/referate/Geschichte/22/Ars-Amatoria--1-Buch-reon.php

09-03-2013 http://www.rhm.uni-koeln.de/137/Schmidt.pdf

11-03-2013 http://de.sci.geschichte.narkive.com/aS2fijoI/caesar-venus

              http://www.geschkult.fu-berlin.de/e/klassarch/projekte/erice/index.html

13-03-2013 http://www.etymonline.com/index.php?term=Venus

14-03-2013 http://novaroma.org/nr/Venus_Verticordia

29-03-2013 http://de.academic.ru/dic.nsf/mythologisches/4073/Mavors

              http://ancienthistory.about.com/od/mgodsandgoddesses/g/062509RomanWarGodMars.htm

02-04-2013 http://antonelloriommidisegni.blogspot.de/2009/04/la-danza-dei-salii-sacerdoti-di-marte.html

07-04-2013 http://www.heinrich-tischner.de/22-sp/7sprv/woche/gr-rom.htm

10-04-2013 http://www.hermes-astrologie.com/history1.htm

11-04-2013 http://www.paulyonline.brill.nl/entries/der-neue-pauly-iuppiter-e603790

25-09-2013 http://www.romlive.de/pantheon/

30-09-2013 http://www.duden.de/rechtschreibung/Tierkreis

09-10-2013 http://www.wortmagier.de/img/werk/1/2.pdf

21-10-2013 http://www.heinrich-tischner.de/22-sp/2wo/wort/alt/v/venia.htm

30-10-2013 http://www.britannica.com/EBchecked/topic/625655/Venus

10-11-2013 http://www.mygeo.info/skripte/skript_bevoelkerung_siedlung/siedl1.htm

              http://www.mygeo.info/skripte/skript_bevoelkerung_siedlung/siedl2.htm

12-11-2013 http://www.thelatinlibrary.com/livy/liv.1.shtml

12-11-2013 http://www.romanoimpero.com/2009/10/il-culto-di-giove.html

15-12-2013 http://www.pascua.de/planetenkinder/mu/mu-mercurius-gesamt.htm

30-12-2013 http://latin_german.deacademic.com/45519/simpulum

08-01-2014 http://penelope.uchicago.edu/Thayer/E/Roman/Texts/secondary/SMIGRA*/Aerarium.html

Astrological German website of the author: https://www.sonnenastro.de
Email: HGoos@Sonnenastro.de

All Books by Hannelore Goos are published by Books on Demand, Norderstedt, Germany.

Availiable in every book shop.

Recommended:

Gods of the Germanic Peoples
From Roman Times to the Viking Age

This two-volume work offers detailed alphabetic listed information about over 270 deities of the Germanic peoples and covers the time from the Roman Era – the first centuries CE in which the Roman Empire enfolded large parts of the territories of Europe where Germanic peoples lived – up to the Viking Age.

Except for a worldwide available B/W edition also a beautiful color edition exists with 87 great illustrations in full color; **this color edition can be ordered only from shops in Germany, like the shop of the publisher at https://www.bod.de/buchshop/ or http://www.fairbuch.de/**

A few random pages can be viewed at:
http://www.chaosowl.net/view-k.pdf

Color print edition € 27,--/Vol.	Grayscale print edition € 17,--/Vol.
Volume 1: ISBN 978-3-7347-3201-0	Volume 1: ISBN 978-3-7347-3396-3
Volume 2: ISBN 978-3-7347-3391-8	Volume 2: ISBN 978-3-7347-3397-0

The contents of "Germanic Magic" incorporates related passed down fragments on magic but actually it is rather a modern system of rune magic, based on current magical principles. And although Germanic Magic is more that just runic magic and that indeed is implemented, the core of the work are the runes of the Elder Futhark.

The book is split up into three parts. The science-based "Part 1" deals with the runes that are preserved in finds, such as inscriptions in stones. A fair selection of these finds, including pictures, is presented and elaborated in transcriptions and possible meanings. The basis of "Part 2" is mythology and gives an overview of myths, poems and sagas in which runes appear and quite a few of these sources are quoted. In addition, these two parts also summarize historical and mythological backgrounds on Germanic Peoples and some of their deities who are connected here to runes..

These two sections on history and mythology are a kind of restricting basis for "Part 3", the principal part, where theory and practice of a current system of rune magic is given. This is presented in a way, that it also can be taken as an initial learning pathway for those who want to go the 'magical way' to become a rune magician.